a leader's guide to

Sex Lies & ...The Truth™

A Biblical Character-Building, Abstinence-Based Program

FOCUS ON THE FAMILY
EDUCATIONAL RESOURCES

Colorado Springs, Colorado

ACKNOWLEDGMENTS

Focus on the Family wishes to thank those who made this leader's guide possible:

All scripture taken from HOLY BIBLE, NEW INTERNATIONAL VERSION.® Copyright © 1973, 1978, 1984 by International Bible Society. Used by permission of Zondervan Publishing House. All rights reserved.

United Technologies for the use of their poem "Will the Real You Please Stand Up," copyright © 1983 United Technologies Corp.

Educational Guidance Institute Inc. for the use of their chart "The Human Person," from *Foundations for Family Education,* copyright © 1991 Educational Guidance Institute Inc., 9275 So. Walter Reed Dr., Suite 4, Arlington, VA 22204.

Maureen Duran, Dr. Reed Bell and Dr. Paul Reiser for their contributions to the content of the leader's guide.

Our thanks go to the many doctors and health care providers who have scrutinized this leader's guide for its content and medical accuracy, and to the following for their confirmation of biblical accuracy: the Rev. Allen Fischer of Immanuel Bible Church, Springfield, Va., the Rev. William Scroggins of Cornerstone Christian Church, Tuscaloosa, Ala., the Rev. Don Wilkins of New Paris Missionary Church, New Paris, Ind., Pastor Chris Hodges of New Life Church, Colorado Springs, Colo., and Mr. Bob Laird of the Diocese of Arlington, Arlington, Va.

Martha Long of An Educated Choice Inc. for contributions to the content of the leader's guide.

A LEADER'S GUIDE TO SEX, LIES AND . . . THE TRUTH ™

FOREWORD

Thank you for your interest in Focus on the Family's *Sex, Lies and . . . the Truth* video/study guide package. We're grateful for your desire to bring the abstinence message to teens in your church, school or organization. I hope that it will help you teach and minister more effectively to young people.

It is surely a sign of the times that I am even writing this foreword to a leader's guide on sexual abstinence for *Christian* teens. Just ten years ago, I would never have imagined the need for such a manual! While the experts can tell us how we got here from the not-so-long-ago day when the majority of "good Christian kids" didn't experiment sexually, I'm not sure that I'd believe it. But the sad fact is, we *are* here. And we must act quickly and decisively to expose the safe-sex myth, counteract the negative peer pressure, and promote the truth—premarital sex is both morally wrong and physically risky.

Interestingly, the more I speak with believers across the country, the more convinced I become that we—the church, pastors, teachers and parents—don't realize just how promiscuous Christian kids are. Lest you think I am exaggerating, one church denomination's recent study of teenagers from the most conservative homes revealed these startling findings:

- 31 percent of the boys and 26 percent of the girls between 16 and 19 years of age had lost their virginity.
- An additional 25 percent said they would have intercourse if the conditions were right.
- In the 12- to 15-year age group, 9 percent of females and 20 percent of males had already had intercourse.[1]

If that doesn't shock you, perhaps this will: According to a study conducted by Josh McDowell, *43 percent of teenagers attending evangelical or fundamental churches had experienced sexual intercourse by age 19.*[2]

Make no mistake, Christian youth are at risk in our permissive culture, and the situation is probably going to get worse. That's why Focus on the Family developed this package. It's aim is to present a relevant, credible, biblical case for teen sexual abstinence—to remind young Christians of God's explicit standards for sexual purity.

In developing *Sex, Lies and . . . the Truth,* we have gone to great lengths to ensure both its biblical integrity and its scientific accuracy. The content has been reviewed by medical authorities and biblical scholars. And, though we've done our best to make the information understandable, provocative and palatable to teens, we have not compromised God's clear prohibition of sexual activity outside the bonds of marriage. You can rely on this guide to present a convincing argument for abstinence.

Again, thank you for your interest in *Sex, Lies and . . . the Truth*. It is a privilege to join with you in this important work of ministering to young people. If you have comments or questions about this package, feel free to contact us.

H.B. London Jr., Pastor
Vice President, Ministry Outreach

1. "Sex and the Nazarene Teen," Mark Graham, *Herald of Holiness,* May 1993, p. 47
2. "Speaker Tells Teens to Just Say No to Sex," Adelle M. Banks, *The Orlando Sentinel Tribune,* July 14, 1993, p. D8.

a leader's guide to

Sex Lies & ...The Truth™

A Biblical Character-Building, Abstinence-Based Program

TABLE OF CONTENTS

A Note to the Leader

Welcome to *Sex, Lies and . . . the Truth,* a biblical character-building, abstinence-based video program that seeks to increase our youths' understanding of sexuality as a normal, healthy and lifelong aspect of human development. You will find that it approaches sexuality by seeking an understanding of the six developmental areas of the human person: intellectual, emotional, social, spiritual, moral and physical. Since the sexual decision-making process impacts all six areas of human development, one area of development should not be addressed without addressing the other five.

The building and strengthening of character is crucial to a child's development. Good judgment, courage, fairness and self-control are the four primary qualities promoted throughout this program. These qualities are the vehicles that enable children to understand why sexuality fits within the context of marriage. It is safe to say that most parents and youth leaders want these qualities taught to children. William Kilpatrick, author of the book *Why Johnny Can't Tell Right From Wrong,* points out that "we must return to the proven model of character education, with its emphasis on good examples and good habits of behavior." When children learn to practice self-control, exercise good judgment, and are fair and courageous, their self-esteem blossoms and they mature into healthy, responsible adults. As with any material on sex education, age appropriateness is very important. This leader's guide was developed for middle and high schoolers. However, it is up to your discretion and that of the parents as to which activities and take-home sheets are most appropriate for your group.

In a group, a leader instructs teens at different developmental levels. Instruction in family life education needs to be clear and concise, especially with respect to the sexual decision-making process. We need to help teenagers develop a sense of awareness and uniqueness, show them that they can express their sexuality in ways other than becoming sexually active and let them know they are allowed to practice or regain their sexual self-control. In a study reported in *Family Planning Perspectives* (1990), more than 1,000 sexually active girls, ages 16 and younger, were asked on what topic they wanted more information. Eighty-four percent checked the item "how to say no without hurting the other person's feelings."[1]

Most teens are not looking for a sexual relationship. They are looking for intimacy, someone who likes them for who they are, without sexual involvement. Research reported by the *Journal of Adolescent Health Care* states, "The strongest motivations for adolescent sexuality are the emotional and psychological needs to love and be loved . . . Often, the physical enjoyment of sex is not an important motivation, particularly among young adolescents."[2]

Changing Behavior

As a youth leader, you are a behavioral change agent. You have the tremendous opportunity to try to change the behavior of children who engage in unhealthy actions, such as drugs, alcohol and promiscuity. Tragically, as reported in the *Journal of Adolescent Health Care* (1991), "the rates of adverse sexual consequences among our teenagers have not fallen and risky sexual behaviors seem to be increasing."[3] *Family Planning Perspectives*, the official publication of Planned Parenthood's research arm says, "HIV/AIDS instruction is not associated with less risky sexual behavior."[4]

We cannot stand by and allow children to continue risk-taking behaviors. By arming children with cessation and refusal skills, they will be able to combat misinformation from peers and misleading messages from the media and the entertainment industry. Former Secretary of Education William Bennett states, "We should explain to children that sex is tied to the deepest recesses of the personality. We should tell the truth; we should describe reality. We should explain that sex involves complicated feelings and emotions. Some of these are ennobling, and some of them—let us be truthful—can be cheapening of one's own finer impulses and cheapening to others."[5]

Family Involvement

Whenever possible, work together with the family to help a child overcome a harmful behavior. Although it may be difficult and sometimes seem impossible, for the sake of the child, modifying the unhealthy behavior should always be pursued. *Parental involvement should be sought in any abstinence-based program, because parents have the primary responsibility for educating their children about sexuality.*

Often you may feel that parental involvement is minimal or non-existent. In some cases this is true. However, parents have always been the strongest factor in helping their children refrain from drugs, alcohol and promiscuity. The most important predictor of sexual activity is the stability of the family.[6] Family structure is an important factor in learning self-restraint. Data indicate that the environment in which a child grows up (i.e. family, church, school, community and peers) is an important predictor of risky behavior:

> The protective role of supportive environments during adolescence must be acknowledged and may be critical in developing prevention and intervention programs. Family and peer factors are crucial, with parental behavior and style being important correlates of onset. Increased parental involvement appears to prevent the onset of risk behaviors and mitigates the most negative outcomes of risk behavior.[7]

Both youth leaders and parents must teach the optimum health message. Abstinence education is pregnancy *and* disease prevention, focusing on risk *elimination* and not simply risk *reduction*. **Teaching reality is teaching abstinence.**

Practical Application of the Four Lessons

In the past several years, there has been a renewed interest in the importance of setting sexual standards and building character in family life courses. In *Sex, Lies and . . . the Truth,* the leader offers a clear and concise presentation, moves to a group discussion and concludes with a summary. The basic conclusions of the lessons found in *Sex, Lies and . . . the Truth* remind us that:

- God knows what is best for us. Premarital sex is against God's will and does not have His blessing. This can, in turn, harden a person's heart against Him.

- A person who practices sexual self-control faces a future free of the consequences, guilt, worry and regret over past sexual involvement.

- Premarital sex impacts a person's intellectual, emotional, social, spiritual, moral and physical growth and development.

- Refusal and cessation skills can help protect a person from the consequences of engaging in unhealthy behavior (drugs, alcohol and promiscuity).

- Healthy relationships are based on "unconditional love."

- A person who regains sexual self-control can enjoy tremendous short- and long-term benefits.

TIPS ON USING THIS GUIDE

PLEASE NOTE: The personal pronoun "he" is used throughout each lesson for the sake of brevity and clarity. It is intended to represent both genders, not solely that of the male.

Sex, Lies and . . . the Truth is a one-week, abstinence-based video program designed to teach teens good judgment, courage, fairness and self-control. This biblical character-building program provides teens with necessary information to understand their sexuality and empowers them to make healthy decisions.

Each of the lessons contains:

- objectives and overviews
- supplemental materials and visual aids
- a list of vocabulary words
- suggested activities and questions
- parent/teen activity handouts
- scripture reference sheets

The study guide is filled with effective and tested age-appropriate activities. The information contained in the lessons is extremely valuable for both pre-teens and teens. Remember, your enthusiasm and motivation are contagious and contribute greatly to the effectiveness of the material.

According to Piaget, the teenager is moving from a concrete to an abstract thinker. Teenagers are not adults. Therefore, you will find many of the abstract concepts are illustrated in a concrete manner. This method will help them internalize difficult concepts.

Each lesson is approximately 40 to 50 minutes long. Specific time frames are identified for each activity. The beginning of each lesson provides you with information regarding:

- an overview
- specific objectives
- materials, supplies, transparencies and handouts
- vocabulary terms

The *HIV/AIDS in Today's Society* lesson is not numbered for a specific reason. The first four lessons are linked to the *Sex, Lies and . . . the Truth* video, produced by Focus on the Family Films. The HIV/AIDS lesson provides leaders and parents with important discussion material from a health perspective.

BROCHURES

Brochures used in the lessons were developed by the United States Department of Health and Human Services (HHS). To order a free supply for your group, call the Family Life Information Exchange, a division of HHS, at (301) 585-6636. It is recommended that you do this as far in advance as possible. The brochures used are:

- *If You Think Saying "No" Is Tough, Just Wait 'Til You Say "Yes"*

- *You didn't get pregnant. You didn't get AIDS. So why do you feel so bad?*

TRANSPARENCIES

Transparency masters can be found at the end of each lesson. They are excellent teaching tools that you may wish to make copies of to hand out to your group. Also, some are appropriate to copy and attach to the parent/teen activity handout.

PARENT/TEEN ACTIVITY HANDOUTS

The parent/teen activity handouts, located at the end of each lesson, are designed to promote parental involvement and communication. Parents should initial each handout and send it back with their child to the next group meeting.

TAKE-HOME ASSIGNMENTS

Take-home assignments, also found at the end of each lesson, were developed to reinforce the lesson plan and should be completed before the next group meeting.

1 Sex, Love & Marriage

Objectives for teens

1. To be able to understand that human sexuality is based on a person's intellectual, emotional, social, spiritual, moral and physical development.

2. To be able to identify the outcomes and consequences of the sexual decision-making process.

3. To be able to define unconditional love and its role in a marriage relationship.

4. To be able to analyze the problems of a premarital sexual relationship.

Overview

This lesson will teach teens how human sexuality fits within the context of marriage, the advantages of abstinence until marriage and the consequences of choosing to be involved in a sexual relationship.

Materials

- Chalkboard or flip chart
- Overhead projector
- Transparencies
    A. The Human Person
    B. Blank transparency (optional)
    C. Progression of Sexual Feeling With Increase of Physical Intimacy
    D. 14 Key Clues to Distinguishing Infatuation From Love

Handouts

- *If You Think Saying "No" Is Tough, Just Wait 'Til You Say "Yes"* brochure
- Scripture reference sheet
- Parent/teen activity handout
- Take-home assignment

Vocabulary

- adultery
- bonding
- fornication
- human sexuality
- marriage
- moral
- petting
- unconditional love

Reminder: Scripture meanings can be abstract and too difficult for teens to grasp. Therefore, use analogies and appropriate language during interpretations of scripture. Distribute the "Scripture Reference Sheets" to the group. Make sure difficult vocabulary words are defined.

INTRODUCTION

Give the group a brief overview of the lesson by reviewing the following key points:

- Scripture references can support and encourage teens to engage in healthy behaviors.

- Human sexuality is not just physical; it is also an intellectual, emotional, social, spiritual and moral act.

- The consequences of premarital sex can affect many people.

- Lasting relationships are based on unconditional love.

- Physical intimacy, which often results in sexual intercourse (bonding), changes a relationship forever.

"It is God's will that you should be sanctified; that you should avoid sexual immorality; that each of you should learn to control his own body in a way that is holy and honorable . . ." —(1 Thessalonians 4:3,4) God desires all of us to be happy and holy. He provides us with guidelines on sexual morality. He does not want us to suffer the pains and consequences of premarital sex. In discussing the meaning of human sexuality, relate it to the scripture reference.

God is the creator of human life. He intended human sexuality to mean everything that makes a person masculine or feminine. Teenage sexuality did not begin at puberty. Sexuality is the process in which we grow and develop as human beings.

The true meaning of human sexuality has become distorted in today's society. However, it is important for teens to understand sexuality as they move toward mature adulthood.

What is human sexuality? Responses may include: sex, sexual intercourse and body parts. You will find that most responses focus on the physical dimension of the human person. It is essential to communicate that it also involves the intellectual, emotional, social, spiritual and moral parts of our personhood.

ACTIVITY: SEX IS WHAT YOU ARE

TIME: 2 minutes

Ask for a volunteer or choose a teen to answer the following questions:

- What is your name?
- What is your address?
- How tall are you?
- What color are your eyes?
- What is your sex?

Most teens will answer the last question correctly by responding either "male" or "female." They will not say, "Well, I have had sex twice," or "I'm still a virgin." Human sexuality is what makes us male or female. God intends us to use our sexuality in a specific way. **". . . Therefore honor God with your body."**—(1 Corinthians 6:20)

ACTIVITY: IS PHYSICAL MATURITY ENOUGH?

TIME: 5 minutes

Use the "Human Person" transparency to show your teens that humans develop intellectually, emotionally, socially, spiritually, morally *and* physically. Explain that the black outline of the human person represents emotional development. Our emotions permeate *all* areas of human development.

When a person makes a major decision in life, it may affect every area of his development. For instance, if someone decides to use drugs it can affect him intellectually, emotionally, socially, spiritually, morally and physically. The same can be said about the decision to engage in premarital sex, as it can go against a person's academic goals and personal or moral standards.

Most teens have reached physical or reproductive maturity. Ask your teens how mature they feel in *all* the other areas of human development. Remind them physical maturity is attained through time and nutrition, but intellectual, emotional, social, spiritual and moral maturity requires hard work, responsibility, good judgment and self-control. Create group discussion with the following question: "Would it be detrimental if a person became involved in premarital sex or continued having premarital sex when he had not yet matured intellectually, emotionally, socially, spiritually and morally?"

Fornication is an inclusive term referring to all kinds of sexual immorality, including sexual intercourse between two unmarried people. Adultery is sexual intercourse between two people, at least one of whom is married to someone else. Read the following scripture passage to the group: **"Flee from sexual immorality. All other sins a man commits are outside his body, but he who sins sexually sins against his own body. Do you not know that your body is a temple of the Holy Spirit, who is in you, whom you have received from God? You are not your own; you were bought at a price. Therefore honor God with your body."**—(1 Corinthians 6:18-20) God understands that men and women may have strong sexual desires. However, God clearly states that sexual activity and intercourse only within marriage will lead to our happiness.

If a person decides to be sexually active it impairs his relationship with God because he sins against his body which houses the Holy Spirit. Jesus died for our sins, therefore, we need to honor and thank Him by respecting our body and others.

Major life decisions impact a person in many ways. It is important for teens to consider the consequences when making a decision about sex, which can affect all six areas of their growth and maturity.

Men and women were created differently. Young men usually reach their sexual peak many years before a woman.[8] Since God is the creator of all life He understands the strong hormonal drive in men. He gives young men instructions on how to deal with difficult situations in their lives. In the Bible it states, **"How can a young man keep his way pure? By living according to your word . . . I have hidden your word in my heart that I might not sin against you."**—(Psalm 119:9,11) **"Finally, brothers, whatever is true, whatever is noble, whatever is right, whatever is pure, whatever is lovely, whatever is admirable—if anything is excellent or praiseworthy—think about such things."**—(Philippians 4:8) The best defense against sexual temptation is by taking refuge in the Lord's words and promises.

ACTIVITY:
SEXUAL ACTIVITY MAKES SENSE IN MARRIAGE

TIME: 15 minutes

Sexual activity leads to a special bond that helps keep a marital relationship together. Use the transparency "Progression of Sexual Intimacy" to explain to your teens how a spouse's body is prepared for sexual intercourse. Sexual intercourse leads to physical bonding. Because teens are not ready to be involved in a committed sexual relationship during this time of their life, it is important that they refrain from sexual activity. Pose the question: "How does a person feel when a sexual relationship has ended?" Most likely, they will respond with such answers as rejected, disappointed and hurt.

The emotional consequences of premarital sex are due, in part, to the breaking of a physical bond. Verbally illustrate this by explaining to your teens that if they took two pieces of paper and glued them together and let the glue dry, when they tried to separate the sheets they could not make a clean split. Parts of each piece of paper stick to the other.

The same thing occurs in physical bonding. When a couple engages in sexual activity (touching body parts or having sexual intercourse), bonding occurs. The couple is not only giving their bodies but also their entire person to the other. When the relationship ends, the couple cannot make a clean split emotionally. They have given a part of themselves away. Review the six developmental aspects of a human being with your teens to remind them that sexual activity is not just a physical act.

Start group discussion by asking: "Why do couples who engage in premarital sex experience so much jealousy, possessiveness and an attitude of ownership?" An example of this is that of a sexually active couple who goes to a high school dance. The guy may not let his girlfriend dance with any other guys even though she enjoys dancing. Or, the girl may not want her boyfriend to talk to other girls. This is because the sexually active teenager may feel threatened and insecure since the relationship lacks true marital commitment. Without this important element, the relationship can end *very easily* and at *any* time.

Unlike premarital sexual relationships or couples who cohabitate, marriage is quite different. God sets marriage apart as a holy and unequalled event, steadfast in permanence. **"What God has joined together, let man not separate."**—(Mark 10:9) A marriage relationship is an everlasting commitment between God and two other people.

Up until the public wedding ceremony, couples are to exercise self-control and abstain from sexual activity because God has reserved sexual intercourse to be the seal of the marriage relationship. God wants us to recognize the importance of marriage. In Hebrews 13:4 it states **"Marriage should be honored by all, and the marriage bed kept pure, for God will judge the adulterer and all the sexually immoral."** Sexual intercourse within marriage in the sight of God is sacred and is a part of what builds and strengthens a marriage. 1 Thessalonians 4:3-5 states, **"It is God's will that you should be sanctified: that you should avoid sexual immorality; that each of you should learn to control his own body in a way that is holy and honorable, not in passionate lust like the heathen, who do not know God . . ."** God intends for sexual intercourse to be reserved for marriage as a gift between husband and wife.

Sex *demands* commitment. The progression of sexual intimacy is a wonderful event between committed spouses. Sexual self-control can lead to even greater trust in marriage.

Most premarital sexual relationships are not based on unconditional love. Ask the group to define unconditional love. The ability to respect and care for others because they are human beings, despite all imperfections, is a true sign of unconditional love. Challenge them with these questions: "If you want what is best for someone, would you put that person's health or emotional well-being at risk?" "Would you put that person at risk of a sexually transmitted disease (STD)?" Remind them that "No" is a loving and caring response.

ACTIVITY: COMMITTED LOVE OR INFATUATION?

TIME: 10 minutes

Divide teens into four teams. Two teams represent "committed love" and the other two teams represent "infatuation." Have each team come up with a skit representing their theme. Encourage teens to use the characteristics listed under "Committed Love" and "It's Infatuation" on the "14 Key Clues to Distinguish Infatuation From Love" transparency to help them create their role play. Team members should brainstorm and come up with additional suggestions. Then have each team select two individuals to role play relationships based on love or infatuation for the group.

CONCLUSION

We all make mistakes. Teens can fail as well as adults. Regaining control has tremendous benefits. When a person regains self-control he experiences hope, courage and self-esteem. He has learned and earned the ability to feel good about himself. When a person starts over and changes an unhealthy behavior (drugs, alcohol, premarital sex), he learns to care about himself and the well-being of others.

Read aloud the following scripture passage: **". . . put off your old self, which is being corrupted by its deceitful desires; to be made new in the attitude of your minds; and to put on the new self, created to be like God in true righteousness and holiness."**—(Ephesians 4:22-24) Regaining self-control means to put aside unhealthy habits and learn from past mistakes. Start again and wipe the slate clean. A new man created in God's image will find help in God's strength. Read: **"I can do everything through him who gives me strength."**—(Philippians 4:13)

Responsible sexual behavior is based on fidelity, commitment and maturity, placing sexuality within the context of marriage. Responsible sexual behavior, like the video points out, is practicing not "safe sex," but sexual self-control.

Distribute the brochure *If You Think Saying "No" Is Tough, Just Wait 'Til You Say "Yes,"* the parent/teen activity handout, scripture reference sheet and lesson one take-home assignment. Teens should have them completed prior to the next meeting.

SCRIPTURE REFERENCE SHEET

"It is God's will that you should be sanctified; that you should avoid sexual immorality; that each of you should learn to control his body in a way that is holy and honorable . . ." 1 Thessalonians 4:3,4

"Flee from sexual immorality. All other sins a man commits are outside his body, but he who sins sexually sins against his own body. Do you not know that your body is a temple of the Holy Spirit, who is in you, whom you have received from God? You are not your own; you were bought at a price. Therefore honor God with your body." 1 Corinthians 6:18-20

"How can a young man keep his way pure? By living according to your word . . . I have hidden your word in my heart that I might not sin against you." Psalm 119:9,11

"Finally, brothers, whatever is true, whatever is noble, whatever is right, whatever is pure, whatever is lovely, whatever is admirable—if anything is excellent or praiseworthy—think about such things." Philippians 4:8

"Therefore what God has joined together, let man not separate." Mark 10:9, Matthew 19:6

"Marriage should be honored by all, and the marriage bed kept pure, for God will judge the adulterer and all the sexually immoral." Hebrews 13:4

"It is God's will that you should be sanctified: that you should avoid sexual immorality; that each of you should learn to control his own body in a way that is holy and honorable, not in passionate lust like the heathen, who do not know God . . ." 1 Thessalonians 4:3-5

" . . . put off your old self, which is being corrupted by its deceitful desires; to be made new in the attitude of your minds; and to put on the new self, created to be like God in true righteousness and holiness." Ephesians 4:22-24

"I can do everything through him who gives me strength." Philippians 4:13

OVERVIEW

This lesson has emphasized how human sexuality fits within the context of marriage, the advantages of waiting until marriage for sexual intimacy and the consequences of choosing to be involved in a sexual relationship outside of marriage.

SCRIPTURE OBJECTIVE

Teens will understand why God says sensuous activities which lead to sexual intercourse outside of marriage are off limits.

PARENT/TEEN DISCUSSION ACTIVITY

1. Discuss the meaning of the following statement: "A 12-year-old can father a child but he cannot be a man to the child."

2. Discuss with your teen why sexual activity demands commitment within the context of marriage.

TAKE-HOME ASSIGNMENT

When a person has sex with others, he gives part of himself away during every sexual experience. In the video, abstinence speaker Miles McPherson said, "Every time you have sex, you give your heart away and what is left?" In a marriage, a couple promises to each other, and to society, that they are willing to make a commitment to stay together. The couple's public commitment is not the same as a couple simply telling one another that they are committed. A premarital sexual relationship is easier to walk away from than a marriage.

DIRECTIONS

1. John and Steve are friends. Steve has been dating Cindy for about a month. He tells John that he thinks he is in love. John isn't quite sure his friend is being realistic about the relationship. What questions can John ask Steve to help him see whether it is infatuation or committed love?

2. Make two lists. One should consist of the reasons why a person would engage in premarital sex with someone. The other list should contain the possible physical and emotional consequences a person may experience, even with just one sexual partner. Compare the two lists. Based upon the comparison, should a person still take the risk and have sex? Why or why not?

The Human Person

Intellectual:

The human person thinks about issues and ideas and makes decisions about his life. Humans have an intellect and a will—the ability to choose.

Moral:

All persons must face the questions concerning good and bad, right and wrong. They must live their life according to a moral code.

Spiritual:

We should all work toward becoming more like Christ on a daily basis. This includes following the commandments set forth in the Bible, seeking God's will and spending time in His Word.

Physical:

The body is the physical structure which houses us. It grows and matures more quickly than the rest of our person.

Emotional:

Emotions (feelings) permeate our whole person. The mature person is one who controls his emotions.

Social:

Each person is part of a community. He learns to interact with others, develop friendships and work to benefit others as well as himself.

The human person must always be considered as a whole—never in parts.

(© 1991 Educational Guidance Institute Inc., 927 S. Walter Reed Dr., Suite 4, Arlington, VA 22204.)

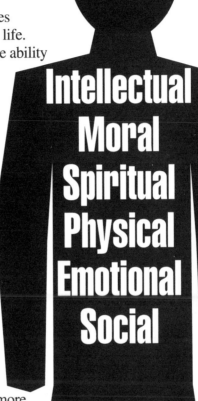

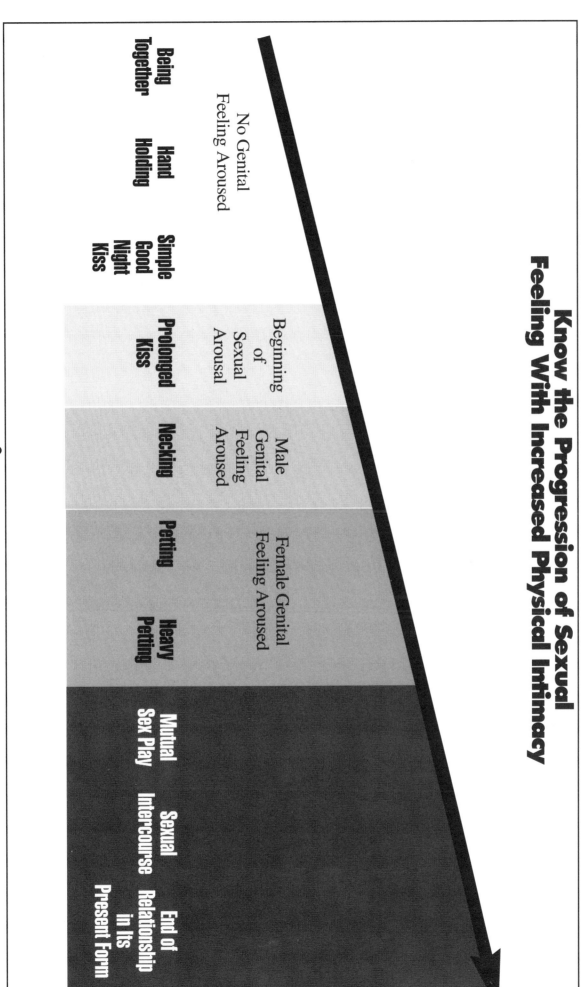

Clues to Distinguish Infatuation From Love

CLUES	CHARACTERISTICS	
Questions to Ask	**It's Infatuation**	**It's Love**
1. What is your main interest? What attracts you most?	The nature of attraction: physical; What responds to the five senses	The total personality: What's in the intellectual, emotional, social, spiritual, moral and physical being
2. How did the romance start?	Fast (hours or days)	Slowly (months or years); Took time to grow
3. What effect does the romance have on your personality?	Highs and lows, can keep you consumed	Organized, constructive, you're a better person
4. How does it end?	Fast, unless the couple has been sexually active	Slowly, takes a long time; You may never be quite the same
5. How do you view each other?	You live in a one-person world. You see the other as faultless, or idealize him or her	You add the new relationship to former ones. You are more realistic, admitting others' faults, but love them anyway
6. What does distance or periods of long separation do to the relationship?	Creates stress; Can wither away, break up	Survives; May even grow stronger. Committed to working through the distance
7. How do quarrels affect the romance?	They get more frequent, more severe and will kill the relationship	When they happen the couple tries to work out disagreements
8. How do you feel about and refer to your relationship?	Much use of the I/Me/My; He/Him/His; She/Her/Hers; Little feeling of oneness	Speaks of We/Us/Our; Feel and think as a unit, a pair; Togetherness
9. What's your ego response to the other?	Mainly selfish, restrictive; "What does this do for me?"	Mainly unselfish, releasing; Concerned equally for the other
10. What's your overall attitude toward the other?	Attitude of taking	Attitude of giving, sharing; Wants to serve the other's needs and wants
11. What is the effect of jealousy?	More frequent, more possessive	Less frequent, has a base of trust
Characteristics to look for:	**Infatuation**	**Committed Love**

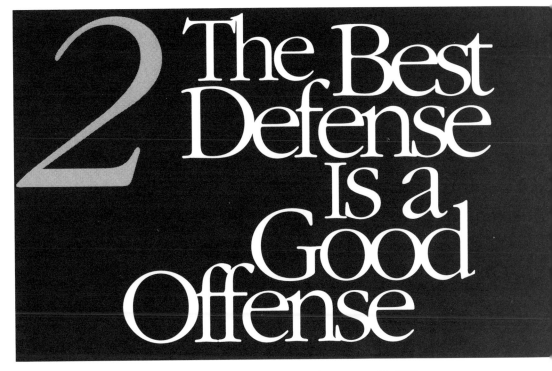

2 The Best Defense Is a Good Offense

Critical Thinking Skills

Objectives for teens

1. To identify negative peer pressure statements.
2. To learn how to say "no" to risk-taking behaviors, including drugs, alcohol and premarital sex.
3. To discuss how premarital sex can alter a person's future.
4. To analyze the messages of the media and music.

Overview

This lesson will teach teens how to effectively say "no" to behaviors that put them "at risk" and the consequences of immediate gratification. In the second part of the lesson, teens will learn how to critically review and assess media messages that promote recreational sex, unhealthy behavior and a distorted portrayal of love.

Materials

• One sheet of paper for each teen
• Chalkboard or flip chart
• Overhead projector

Transparencies

• The Media Message: Healthy or Unhealthy?
• "I Want Your Sex" by George Michael

Handouts

• Worksheet: The Best Defense Is a Good Offense
• Scripture reference sheet
• Parent/teen activity handout
• Take-home assignment
• The Media Message: Healthy or Unhealthy?

Vocabulary

• Desensitize
• Immediate gratification
• Infatuation
• Media
• Refusal skills
• Standards

Reminder: Scripture meanings can be abstract and too difficult for teens to grasp. Therefore, use analogies and appropriate language during interpretations of scripture. Distribute the "Scripture Reference Sheets" to the group. Make sure difficult vocabulary words are defined.

INTRODUCTION

Give the group a brief overview of the lesson by reviewing the following key points:

- Refusal skills protect teens from physical and emotional problems associated with drugs, alcohol and premarital sex.

- Premarital sex can change a person's goals and dreams.

- Developing relationships is an important part of adolescence. But teens don't have to risk their health to be accepted or liked by others.

- Sex sells. Movie producers portray a glamorous image of sex outside of marriage. They do not provide us with the all the facts and consequences surrounding premarital sex.

- Much of the music that teens listen to defines love as a romantic feeling.

Many people have a hard time knowing what is right and wrong when it comes to dating and relationships. God's moral standards leave us with no gray area. He realizes how difficult it can be when we interact with people who have feelings and thoughts which are different from our own. However, by providing us with clear standards of dating and marriage, God helps us know what is right and wrong.

In the video, Anthony Munoz, from the Cincinnati Bengals, said, "The best defense is a good offense!" One important way to build a good offense is to have a set of standards. Standards are guidelines that help a person decide what is right or wrong. Setting standards in advance can protect a person from unforeseen consequences.

To illustrate this, ask your group the following questions: "If a person decides not to cheat on tests and not allow others to copy from his test or paper, what is he protecting himself from?" (Responses may include: being caught by the teacher, receiving a "zero" for a grade, or getting kicked out of school.) "If a person decides not to drink and drive, what is he protecting himself from?" (Responses may include: being involved in an accident, killing himself and others, or having his license revoked.)

Setting standards or moral guidelines can help teens avoid the problems associated with any destructive behavior including drugs, alcohol and premarital sex. We find the most fundamental moral principles in our society in the Ten Commandments of the Old Testament (Exodus 20:2-17, Deuteronomy 5:6-21) and the two greatest commandments of the New Testament (Matthew 22:37-39). The gospel stories are filled with specific examples of how Christ applied the principles and made them real and applicable to our lives. It is not enough, however, to have a set of standards. We need to *apply* these standards. Teens need to be able to explain why they think and feel the way they do.

God clearly tells teenagers how they must act. In 2 Timothy 2:22, it says, **"Flee the evil desires of youth, and pursue righteousness, faith, love and peace, along with those who call on the Lord out of a pure heart."** Setting standards enables teens to avoid compromising situations. Standards protect a teenager from painful memories, guilt, rejection, fear and frustration which usually accompany promiscuity.

Everyone lives with negative peer pressure. Adults, teens and children face different types of pressure from their peers. We can battle negative peer pressure by responding to it in a positive and assertive manner. God states the consequences of people who follow the crowd and engage in unhealthy behaviors. **"Do not be deceived: God cannot be mocked. A man reaps what he sows. The one who sows to please his sinful nature, from that nature will reap destruction; the one who sows to please the Spirit, from the Spirit will reap eternal life."**—(Galatians 6:7,8)

ACTIVITY:
THE BEST DEFENSE IS A GOOD OFFENSE

TIME: 15 minutes

Distribute the "The Best Defense Is a Good Offense" worksheet. Allow the teens to complete the worksheet by themselves. Next, divide teens into teams of six and assign a spokesperson for each. Have teens take turns within their team reading their *best* response for each "line" to the team members. Ask them to decide which team member has the best response for each "line." Have each spokesperson share with the entire group the best six lines from the Drug and Alcohol and the Premarital Sex sections. **No criticism allowed!**

Teens can use refusal skills in a serious or humorous manner to respond to negative peer pressure statements. Whatever the response, they need to follow through on their decision to say "no."

If a person loses a boyfriend or girlfriend because he or she did not want to participate in a risk-taking behavior (drugs, alcohol, smoking or sex), then that friend was not a friend in the first place. Remind the teens that LOVE WANTS WHAT IS BEST FOR THE OTHER PERSON. Friendship is based on mutual respect and that includes respect for one's beliefs and feelings without continued pressure.

Teenagers who are willing to stand up and say "no" to drugs, alcohol and premarital sex may not be liked by everyone. **"Enter through the narrow gate. For wide is the gate and broad is the road that leads to destruction, and many enter through it. But small is the gate and narrow the road that leads to life, and only a few find it."**—(Matthew 7:13,14) **"Blessed are those who are persecuted because of righteousness, for theirs is the kingdom of heaven. Blessed are you when people insult you, persecute you and falsely say all kinds of evil against you because of me."**—(Matthew 5:10,11)

Our future has a lot to do with the habits we form in the middle school and high school years. If teens will *not* say "no" to pressures to participate in drugs, alcohol and/or premarital sex, it will affect their future. Remind them to ask themselves, "What will happen to my future goals and dreams if I don't say no?"

ACTIVITY: MY FUTURE MATTERS [9]

TIME: 15 minutes

Hand each teen a sheet of paper and ask them to fold it in half, then in half again. When the paper is open, there should be four equally divided parts. Using the creases in the paper, have them tear their papers into four equal-sized sheets.

On one sheet of paper, write the number "1" on the top right hand corner. On a second sheet of paper, write the number "4" on the top right hand corner. On a third sheet of paper write the number "8" on the top right hand corner. On the last sheet of paper, write the number "12." The numbers 1, 4, 8 and 12 represent the number of years from today's date.

Have them write one goal or dream that they would like to accomplish 1, 4, 8 and 12 years from now on their corresponding sheet of paper. Names should not be included on the sheets. Collect all four sheets of paper from each teen and put them in a bag or other container.

Ask a volunteer to pick one sheet from the container. On the board, write the year and goal written on the paper. Continue this procedure until the board is filled with the teens' goals and dreams. Then, ask the group the following question: "If a teenager becomes sexually active or continues being sexually involved, how could their goals and dreams be affected?"

Discuss how the goals on the board can be affected by premarital sex. If time allows, erase the board and continue the procedure using different goals which have not been picked out of the container.

Teens who do not strive for their goals and dreams usually live only for the moment. This is why it is important for teens to have a set of standards and goals for their lives.

God sets us straight on whom we should follow. **"Do you not know that the wicked will not inherit the kingdom of God? Do not be deceived: Neither the sexually immoral nor idolaters nor adulterers nor male prostitutes nor homosexual offenders nor thieves nor the greedy nor drunkards nor slanderers nor swindlers will inherit the kingdom of God. And that is what some of you were. But you were washed, you were sanctified, you were justified in the name of the Lord Jesus Christ and by the Spirit of our God."**—(1 Corinthians 6:9-11) It *is* possible to change the hearts and minds of teenagers who are living immoral lives. It is through our example that we best illustrate how Jesus actually lives within us.

ACTIVITY:
THE MESSAGE: HEALTHY OR UNHEALTHY

TIME: 20 minutes

Use "The Message: Healthy or Unhealthy" transparency to analyze the lyrics your teens brought to the group. As an example, you can start with some lyrics from "I Want Your Sex" by George Michael (these can be found in the back of this lesson). (Note: You should read and screen all lyrics for content ahead of time.) Have one teen read the section of the song at a time and ask the group to answer the questions on the transparency.

Developing a critical eye toward media messages will prevent teens from becoming too desensitized. The media bombard young adults with messages communicating that everyone is having sex, sex sells and sex is everywhere. Teens will feel good about sexual abstinence when they are able to discern the difference between healthy and unhealthy media messages. Remind them that they have the power to change the TV channel or switch radio stations.

God gives us a clear understanding on the necessary steps we must take to avoid sexually explicit materials. In Psalm 119:9,11 it states, **"How can a young man keep his way pure? By living according to your word . . . I have hidden your word in my heart that I might not sin against you."** In Job 31:1 it also states, **"I made a covenant with my eyes not to look lustfully at a girl."** Men and women can protect themselves from falling into a state of temptation by knowing and following God's laws on morality and by not entertaining sexual thoughts that enter their mind. In Psalm 101:2,3 it states, **". . . I will walk in my house with a blameless heart. I will set before my eyes no vile thing . . ."** In today's world it is almost impossible not to see sexually explicit materials. Television writers and advertising companies make millions of dollars exploiting men's and women's bodies for profit. However, by avoiding pornography and other places where the human body is exploited (strip joints, topless bars, NC-17 movies), and keeping a critical eye toward media messages, you can protect your heart and mind.

James 1:14-15 states, **". . . but each one is tempted when, by his own evil desire, he is dragged away and enticed. Then, after desire has conceived, it gives birth to sin; and sin, when it is full-grown, gives birth to death."**

Temptation is a wish to gratify a "legal desire in an illegal way." But temptation is not sin until the will says, "Do it!" Another way to view it: temptation is the devil knocking at the door and sin occurs when you open the door and invite him in. It is possible to yield to temptations other than outright sexual activity. Satan may tempt us to dwell on unclean thoughts, urging us to replay them in our minds and corrupting our thought life. By yielding to his prompting, we willfully sin.

In Matthew 5:28, Jesus doesn't condemn the spontaneous charge a man gets when an attractive woman walks by. That in and of itself is just fine—after all, He *created* that excitement. It's your *attitude* that Jesus is concerned with. If a brief thought of appreciation turns into an erotic daydream or fantasy; if you purposely look at another person to be aroused; if you enjoy viewing pornography; if you think of another with sexual intentions; if you plan the "forbidden"—this is sin.

It doesn't matter if you never get around to the actual sexual act. If you've played it out in your mind, you've sinned and need to be reminded that Jesus *commands* us to control our thought life. We can't prevent the illicit desire, but we can prevent the conscious, willful acts that flow from it.

CONCLUSION

At some point in time we are all given the opportunity to go *with* or *against* the crowd. When a person holds tightly to his standards and makes the decision to resist peer pressure, he strengthens his self-esteem. Remind the group that self-esteem is *earned*, not just learned. In today's world, the ability to say "no" can literally save lives. God is waiting to provide us with the courage and strength we need to overcome any external or internal pressure we may experience.

Distribute the parent/teen activity handout, scripture reference sheet and take-home assignment. The teen should have them completed prior to the next meeting.

SCRIPTURE REFERENCE SHEET

"Flee the evil desires of youth, and pursue righteousness, faith, love and peace, along with those who call on the Lord out of a pure heart." 2 Timothy 2:22

"You shall not commit adultery. You shall not steal. You shall not give false testimony against your neighbor. You shall not covet you neighbor's wife. You shall not set your desire on your neighbor's house or land, his manservant or maidservant, his ox or donkey, or anything that belongs to your neighbor." Deuteronomy 5:18-21 (Also see Exodus 20:14-17)

"'. . . Love the Lord your God with all your heart and with all your soul and with all your mind.' This is the first and greatest commandment. And the second is like it: 'Love your neighbour as yourself.'" (Matthew 22:37-39).

"Do not be deceived: God cannot be mocked. A man reaps what he sows. The one who sows to please his sinful nature, from that nature will reap destruction; the one who sows to please the Spirit, from the Spirit will reap eternal life." Galatians 6:7,8

"Enter through the narrow gate. For wide is the gate and broad is the road that leads to destruction, and many enter through it. But small is the gate and narrow is the road that leads to life, and only a few find it." Matthew 7:13,14

"Blessed are those who are persecuted because of righteousness, for theirs is the kingdom of heaven. Blessed are you when people insult you, persecute you and falsely say all kinds of evil against you because of me." Matthew 5:10,11

"Do you not know that the wicked will not inherit the kingdom of God? Do not be deceived: Neither the sexually immoral nor idolaters nor adulterers nor male prostitutes nor homosexual offenders nor thieves nor the greedy nor drunkards nor slanderers nor swindlers will inherit the kingdom of God. And that is what some of you were. But you were washed, you were sanctified, you were justified in the name of the Lord Jesus Christ and by the Spirit of our God." 1 Corinthians 6:9-11

"How can a young man keep his way pure? By living according to your word . . . I have hidden your word in my heart that I might not sin against you." Psalm 119:9,11

"I made a covenant with my eyes not to look lustfully at a girl." Job 31:1

". . . I will walk in my house with a blameless heart. I will set before my eyes no vile thing . . ." Psalm 101:2,3

". . . but each one is tempted when, by his own evil desire, he is dragged away and enticed. Then, after desire has conceived, it gives birth to sin; and sin, when is full-grown, gives birth to death." James 1:14-15

But I tell you that anyone who looks at a woman lustfully has already committed adultery with her in his heart." Matthew 5:27,28

THE BEST DEFENSE IS A GOOD OFFENSE

Drugs and Alcohol

Write two responses for each "line."

1. Everyone's doing it!

1a. _____

1b. _____

2. What's the big deal?

2a. _____

2b. _____

3. Aw, come on, have one.

3a. _____

3b. _____

4. Are you scared?

4a. _____

4b. _____

5. You've tried it before, why not try it again?

5a. _____

5b. _____

Premarital Sex

Write two responses for each "line."

1. I thought we loved each other.

1a. _____

1b. _____

2. I'll use protection.

2a. _____

2b. _____

3. Let me show you how much I love you.

3a. _____

3b. _____

4. We're committed to each other.

4a. _____

4b. _____

5. I'll only go as far as you want me to.

5a. _____

5b. _____

6. We've done it before, why can't we do it again?

6a. _____

6b. _____

OVERVIEW

This lesson has emphasized how teens can effectively say "no" to risk-taking behavior and avoid the future consequences of immediate gratification. They have also learned how to critically analyze the media to screen out messages that promote recreational sex, unhealthy behaviors and a distorted portrayal of human sexuality.

SCRIPTURE OBJECTIVE

Teens will be able to identify God's moral laws on sexual immorality and impurity and the importance of God's protection.

PARENT/TEEN DISCUSSION ACTIVITY

1. Parent:
   Discuss ways adults may experience negative peer pressure. How do you cope with peer pressure?

2. Parent and teen:
   Discuss how premarital sex can jeopardize a person's future goals.

   Review your lesson two take-home assignment with your parent. How would your parent rate the song you chose? Use the questionnaire to record their response.

THE MEDIA'S MESSAGE: HEALTHY OR UNHEALTHY

Questions

Answers

	Question	YES	NO
1.	Does the song or television show promote or assume premarital sex?	____	____
2.	Are the words or actions based primarily on feelings?	____	____
3.	Is marriage portrayed as a respected and desirable vocation?	____	____
4.	Are courage, self-control and good judgment promoted?	____	____
5.	Is secrecy promoted?	____	____
6.	Are there harmful consequences in the words or actions being promoted or assumed?	____	____
7.	Do the words or actions promote a promising future for teenagers?	____	____
8.	Do the words or actions promote immediate gratification?	____	____
9.	Do the words or actions confuse "love" with infatuation, sex or romance?	____	____
10.	If you were a parent, would you want your teenager to listen to this song or watch this program?	____	____

Explain Your Answer

_____

_____

_____

_____

_____

_____

_____

_____

_____

_____

_____

THE MEDIA'S MESSAGE: HEALTHY OR UNHEALTHY
Questions

1. Does the song or television show promote or assume premarital sex?

2. Are the words or actions based primarily on feelings?

3. Is marriage portrayed as a respected and desirable vocation?

4. Are courage, self-control and good judgment promoted?

5. Is secrecy promoted?

6. Are there harmful consequences in the words or actions being promoted or assumed?

7. Do the words or actions promote a promising future for teenagers?

8. Do the words or actions promote immediate gratification?

9. Do the words or actions confuse "love" with infatuation, sex or romance?

10. If you were a parent, would you want your teenager to listen to this song or watch this program?

TAKE-HOME ASSIGNMENT

Today you learned that many media messages are distorted and misleading. It is important for a person to be able to differentiate between reality and fantasy when listening to music, watching television or reading advertisements. There are several questions you can ask yourself when you listen, watch or read different forms of the media:

- Is sex being used to sell this product?

- What is the message trying to convey?

For example, "If you buy this car, sexy women will want to be with you" or "If you wear this perfume, guys will chase you around the block."

- What is the reality of the message?

For example, "This beer commercial shows everyone laughing and having a good time, but you never see anyone with a hangover or getting sick the next day." "A television show gives the impression a couple has been sexually active, but you never see the partner going to the local health clinic because he is experiencing a burning sensation when he urinates due to an STD."

- Is this message increasing my desire for sexual pleasures?

There is nothing wrong with temptations. The trouble starts when you "add fuel to the fire" by surrounding yourself with visual stimulation. Pornography is a perfect example of this. Pornography is material that arouses sexual excitement. According to research, viewing pornography leads to thinking that sexual fulfillment comes without enduring commitment, marriage is not a lasting and viable institution, spouses are expected to be unfaithful and premarital sex is natural and normal.

You can *change* television and radio stations, *choose* healthy videos and magazines and *ignore* misleading advertisements.

DIRECTIONS

Using the chart "The Media Message: Healthy or Unhealthy," choose a current song or television program and analyze its message by using the chart's questions. Make sure you identify the title of the song or the name of the television program.

I Want Your Sex

by George Michael

There's things that you guess
And things that you know
There's boys you can trust
And girls that you don't
There's little things you hide
And little things that you show
Sometimes you think you're going to get it
But you don't and that's just the way it goes

I swear I won't tease you
Won't tell you no lies
I don't need no Bible
Just look in my eyes
I've waited so long baby
Now that we're friends
Every man's got his patience
And here's where mine ends

I want your sex
I want you
I want your sex
I want your . . . sex

3 Rewarding Relationships

Objective for teens

1. To be able to distinguish between healthy and unhealthy relationships.
2. To be able to identify myths associated with premarital sex and dating.
3. To be able to discuss how sexually active dating relationships have the potential to affect a teen's future spouse and children.
4. To be able to list successful dating and non-dating activities.

Overview

This lesson will teach teens the short- and long-term consequences of certain dating habits. It also discusses how lasting relationships are based on true friendships.

Materials

- Chalkboard or flip chart
- Overhead projector
- Two containers (i.e. small paper bags)
- STD badges (refer to the back of this section for instructions on how to create)
- Prizes for three to six teens (i.e. candy bars)

Transparencies

- Blank transparency (optional)
- Creative Dating and Non-Dating Guidelines

Handouts

- *"You didn't get pregnant. You didn't get AIDS. So why do you feel so bad?"* brochure
- Scripture reference sheet
- Parent/teen activity handout
- Take-home assignment sheet

Vocabulary

- AIDS
- asymptomatic
- chlamydia
- genital herpes
- gonorrhea
- human papillomavirus—HPV/genital warts
- syphilis
- trichomoniasis

Reminder: Scripture meanings can be abstract and too difficult for teens to grasp. Therefore, use analogies and appropriate language during interpretations of scripture. Distribute the "Scripture Reference Sheets" to the group. Make sure difficult vocabulary words are defined.

INTRODUCTION

Give the group a brief overview of the lesson by reviewing the following key points:

- Most young people are not seeking a *sexual* relationship, but rather one based on *intimacy*.

- Premarital sex dramatically changes the dynamics of a couple's relationship.

- Unhealthy dating relationships can, and most often do, have a harmful effect on a teen's future.

- The secret to building a rewarding relationship is to put what is best for the other person ahead of your own needs.

We are created in the image and likeness of God. And it is important to remember that the Holy Spirit dwells within our bodies. Before getting into a tempting situation, ask yourself, *"Would I do this if God was sitting right next to me?"*

Most young people are looking for someone who likes them for who they are and who they can share their thoughts and feelings with. Unfortunately, too many teens find themselves in a sexual relationship for all the wrong reasons.

ACTIVITY: MYTHS SURROUNDING PREMARITAL SEX

TIME: 5 minutes

Ask the group for reasons why young adults engage in premarital sex. List their responses on a chalkboard, flip chart or transparency. Their responses may include:

- curiosity
- peer pressure
- to save a relationship
- to strengthen a relationship
- to prove one's love

Please note: As you conduct the next activity, make sure your teens understand the myths associated with premarital sex.

Dating is an important part of adolescent development. Dating relationships can enable a teenager to grow intellectually, emotionally, socially, spiritually and morally. They give them the opportunity to better understand themselves and others. And, dating guidelines can protect teenagers. If dating guidelines have not been set prior to dating, short- and long-term consequences can occur. Ask your group the following question: "What are some of the short-term consequences of failing to establish dating guidelines in advance?" Responses may include: pregnancy, rejection or guilt. In Colossians 3:5,6 it states, **"Put to death, therefore, whatever belongs to your earthly nature: sexual immorality, impurity, lust, evil desires and greed, which is idolatry. Because of these, the wrath of God is coming."** Romans 12:9-11 states, **"Love must be sincere. Hate what is evil; cling to what is good. Be devoted to one another in brotherly love. Honor one another above yourselves. Never be lacking in zeal, but keep your spiritual fervor, serving the Lord."** The following activity will help your teens consider the long-term consequences of premarital sex as well.

ACTIVITY: DATING CAN AFFECT A COUPLE'S FUTURE[10]

TIME: 20 minutes

Collect all the guys' names and put them in a container. Collect all of the girls' names and put them into a different container. Select one guy and one girl name from each container. Have the two teens come to the front of the group to create dating scenarios where they eventually fall victim to one of the premarital sex myths. Create as many dating scenarios as necessary to dispel these myths. You'll find that your teens will really enjoy this activity.

Before they begin to act out their scenario, randomly give one person from each couple one, two or three STD badges (see sample in back of this lesson). Do not tell them what the badges represent until after their "relationship" ends. Once the relationship ends, inform the couple that the girl or guy with the STD badge(s) has had sex with other people. Have them read the STD inside the badge(s). Then, discuss some signs and symptoms of each disease.

If an STD badge is blank, it may represent an "asymptomatic" condition of an STD. Asymptomatic means that a person may have an STD without seeing or feeling the symptoms. Many STDs go undetected, such as chlamydia. STDs can leave a teenager sterile and, if not treated, they can harm his children during and after childbirth.

*Remind the group that this activity means discussing sexually transmitted diseases that millions of Americans contract every day, and that joking and criticism in this sensitive area are inappropriate.

Examples of Dating Scenarios

1. Leader: Have two teens, one guy and one girl, come forward. Give the guy two STD badges. Tell the group you will explain the meaning of the badges later.

Dating Scenario: Cindy (the girl selected) dates Kevin (the guy selected) for a few weeks during her sophomore year. They decide that physical intimacy will **strengthen their relationship**. Afterward, Kevin loses interest in Cindy because she is no longer a challenge, and they break up.

Leader: Explain to the group that Kevin had sex with two other girls prior to meeting Cindy. Read the names of the STDs or discuss the meaning of asymptomatic. Do not forget to dispel the premarital sex myth by reminding your group of the following:

In disease transmission, every time you have sex with someone, you're not only having sex with that person, but with everyone that person has had sex with in the past.

2. Leader: Give the next selected girl three STD badges.

Dating Scenario: During her junior year, Kathy (the next girl selected) meets Sean (the next guy selected). She falls in love and is certain that he is *the one* for her. Kathy thinks that physical intimacy will **help her determine if Sean really is the right one**. After a few dates, they become sexually active. Soon after, Kathy becomes interested in a different guy in school. Kathy and Sean break up, as physical intimacy could not hold them together.

Leader: Kathy had been sexually involved with three other people before meeting Sean. Read the names of the STDs or discuss the meaning of asymptomatic. Dispel the premarital sex myth.

3. Leader: Give the newly selected girl two STD badges.

Dating Scenario: During her senior year, Paula begins dating Pat. They get along well and spend a lot of time studying together. Prom night approaches. They want to make it a night to remember by **proving their love.** The evening ends with Paula and Pat sleeping together. At first, everything seems great. But in the last few weeks of school, their relationship sours. By the time they graduate, they are no longer speaking to each other.

Leader: Discuss the STDs and dispel the premarital sex myth. Did having sex prove they were in love?

4. Leader: Give the next guy three STD badges.

Dating Scenario: Janet goes to college where she meets Mark. (He is in several of her classes.) They begin dating and over a period of several months, Mark pressures Janet to have sex. Finally, Janet gives in and has sex with Mark **to save the relationship**. Eventually, Janet finds out that Mark is having sex with several other girls and she ends the relationship.

Leader: Discuss the STDs and dispel the premarital sex myth. Did having sex keep the relationship together?

Sexual dating relationships have the potential of affecting teenagers as well as their future spouses and children. If a girl acquires an STD and it goes undetected, she could pass it along to both her spouse and children (as in the case of herpes).

Dating should be a fun and exciting time for a teenager. Group dating tends to provide the most fun because of the number of people involved. Research concludes that **the earlier a teen starts to date, the greater the chances he will get involved in a sexual relationship.** Going steady, or dating one person exclusively, quite often leads to sexual activity and pregnancy. By setting dating guidelines in advance, teens can avoid the consequences of a premarital sexual relationship.

ACTIVITY: CREATIVE DATING

TIME: 20 minutes

Separate the teens into teams. Assign each team a number. The objective of each team is to create a fun and exciting dating or non-dating activity for young adults. Dating or non-dating activities must follow certain guidelines. Use the "Creative Dating and Non-Dating Guidelines" transparency and read aloud each guideline to the team. Explain that if they do not adhere to *all* of the guidelines, their dating activities will be disregarded.

Have each team appoint a spokesperson. Once the dating or non-dating activity is created and completed, the spokesperson will explain to the rest of the group the creative date. On a scrap piece of paper, ask teens to vote for the team with the most creative date. Collect and count the votes. Award a prize to the team with the best date. Rewards could be a candy bar or ice cream money for lunch time.

CONCLUSION

Teens can have a great time on a date without having to face the pressures of having sex. And, dating does not have to be selfish. You can have lots of fun doing things *for* other people. Being creative and working within boundaries are the keys to successful dating. God provides us with dating guidlines. In 1 Corinthians 6:18,19, it states, **"Flee from sexual immorality. All other sins a man commits are outside his body, but he who sins sexually sins against his own body. Do you not know that your body is a temple of the Holy Spirit who is in you, whom you have received from God? . . ."** It is important to keep in mind that while no one is perfect, it is God's desire that we live clean, pure lives. However, if we yield to temptation and fall into sin, God anxiously waits for us to ask His forgiveness to right our relationship with Him.

Distribute the parent/teen activity handout which should include the brochure, *"You didn't get pregnant. You didn't get AIDS. So why do you feel so bad?,"* the scripture reference sheet and the take-home assignment. Request that they are completed prior to the next meeting.

SCRIPTURE REFERENCE SHEET

"Put to death, therefore, whatever belongs to your earthly nature: sexual immorality, impurity, lust, evil desires and greed, which is idolatry. Because of these, the wrath of God is coming." Colossians 3:5,6

"Love must be sincere. Hate what is evil; cling to what is good. Be devoted to one another in brotherly love. Honor one another above yourselves. Never be lacking in zeal, but keep your spiritual fervor, serving the Lord." Romans 12:9-11

"Flee from sexual immorality. All other sins a man commits are outside his body, but he who sins sexually sins against his own body. Do you not know that your body is a temple of the Holy Spirit who is in you, whom you have received from God? You are not your own; you were bought at a price. Therefore honor God with your body." 1 Corinthians 6:18-20

OVERVIEW

This lesson has emphasized the fact that certain dating habits will have short- and long-term consequences. Teens have learned how premarital sex may fool a couple into believing that they have a strong relationship, but lasting relationships are based on true friendship.

SCRIPTURE OBJECTIVE

Teens will be able to understand why God asks us to control our bodies and strive for holiness.

PARENT/TEEN DISCUSSION ACTIVITY

1. Parent:

   Share with your teen some of the dating guidelines you followed and dating or non-dating activities you participated in during your high school years. You may wish to explain the benefits and downfalls of your experiences.

2. Parent and teen:

   Discuss your views on the "premarital sex strengthens relationships" myth.

   Discuss the brochure *"You didn't get pregnant. You didn't get AIDS. So why do you feel so bad?"*

TAKE-HOME ASSIGNMENT

At some point in our lives, we are given the opportunity to go *with* or *against* the crowd. When a person holds strongly to his beliefs or standards, he will not give into peer pressure. Most likely, this person has learned refusal skills, which are important to have, especially when dating.

Learning how to respond to pressure can prevent a date from turning into disaster. You need to learn three quick and easy rules: **state it, sell it** and **move it.**

- **State It:** Say "no" to an idea and state why.
- **Sell It:** Come up with an alternative plan of action.
- **Move It:** Stick to the alternate plan and leave the door open for the other person to follow.

Here's an example of using the state it, sell it and move it strategy:

Story: Bob and Janet are at a party. Bob has been drinking too much. The evening comes to an end and it is time to go home.

Bob: "C'mon, let me drive you home."

Janet: **(State It)** "No, Bob. You're drunk and we could get in an accident or pulled over by the police."

Bob: "Oh, I'm fine. I've driven home hundreds of times this way."

Jane: **(Sell It)** "Why don't I call a cab and we can get your car in the morning? It will be much safer."

Bob: "Don't be scared, nothing is going to happen."

Janet: **(Move It)** "Bob, I'm calling a cab and going home. The risk is not worth it for me. You are free to come with me. I'm asking Billy to take the keys and I'll see you tomorrow."

DIRECTIONS:

Use the "Dating" and "Dressing Room" scenarios and apply the state it, sell it and move it strategy to each one.

DATING SCENARIO

Liz and Kevin are studying in her living room while her parents are at work. While they are studying, Kevin leans over and begins kissing Liz. The couch looks inviting, but Liz knows what might happen if they get "too comfortable."

Kevin: "Liz, nothing is going to happen . . . I promise. I just want to show you how much I care."

Liz: **(State It)** _____

_____

Kevin: "Don't worry, your parents won't be home for hours!"

Liz: **(Sell It)** _____

_____

Kevin: "I thought you cared about me . . ."

Liz: **(Move It)** _____

_____

DRESSING ROOM SCENARIO

Candy is with her friends at the mall. They go into a store and try on clothes. In the dressing room, Jenny puts a pair of shorts in her purse and asks Candy to put a belt in her purse.

Jenny: "C'mon Candy, nothing is going to happen. I've stolen from this store a million times."

Candy: **(State It)** _____

_____

Jenny: "It's just a belt and a pair of shorts! The security tags are off—no one will know!"

Candy: **(Sell It)** _____

_____

Jenny: "I want these shorts. Why should I buy them when I can get them free?"

Candy: **(Move It)** _____

_____

CREATIVE DATING AND NON-DATING GUIDELINES

• Each person involved cannot spend more than $10.

• The activity has to be non-alcoholic and drug-free.

• The activity has to last at least an hour.

• Parental/guardian permission is required.

STD BADGES

To create STD badges, refer to the pattern sample. The circles are four or five inches in diameter. Cut them out and fold each badge on the dotted line so that you cannot see the name of the STD. If you like, draw eyes, a nose and a mouth on the front of each badge.

A total of 10 badges are needed. On the inside of seven badges, write the name of a commonly acquired STD (as described below). The three remaining badges should be left blank, representing either an asymptomatic condition of an STD or no STD at all. (An illustration of these can be found at the end of the lesson.)

STD INFORMATION

SEXUALLY TRANSMITTED DISEASE (STD): A communicable disease which is spread through sexual contact.

ACQUIRED IMMUNODEFICIENCY SYNDROME (AIDS): A disease that compromises the competency of the immune system, characterized by persistent and various opportunistic infections. The causative agent, HIV, is transmitted by body fluids such as blood and semen.

CHLAMYDIA: An infection caused by the most common sexually transmitted microorganism in the United States. Contracted only by intercourse, its primary site of infection is a woman's uterus, tubes and ovaries. This can cause sterility and/or abdominal pain. A woman can receive the infectious organism chlamydia trachomatis from a man during intercourse and carry it in her reproductive organs. An infected woman may experience urethral discharge, burning with urination, an urgency or frequency of urination and pain in the lower abdomen just above the pubic bone. Men who become infected with chlamydia often have no symptoms. As many as 70 percent of all infected men will not even know they have the organism present in the urethra. If there are symptoms, they might include a discharge of pus from the penis and burning with urination.

GENITAL HERPES: The infective virus, herpes simplex type II, is spread by direct contact with someone carrying the virus. This contact may be sexual intercourse, but the virus can be spread by oral contact, so herpes sores on the lips may result from kissing or from oral-genital contact with an infected individual. The common fever blister or "cold sore" is caused by the virus herpes simplex type I. Once the herpes virus gets into the tissues, it is there to stay. An outbreak of herpes can cause enlarged lymph nodes in the groin. Flu-like symptoms may occur in the form of fever and muscle aches. In men, blisters may appear on the penis, the scrotum, or the anus; in women, the sores may be on the vulva, inside the vagina, on the cervix, or in the anal region.

GONORRHEA: A sexually transmitted disease caused by the gonococcus, a pus-producing bacterium that is almost never transmitted any other way than by intercourse. One of the main problems with gonorrhea, as with certain other STDs, is that it can be present and produce no noticeable symptoms. A woman who has contracted gonorrhea from intercourse may not show symptoms for days or even months. Early symptoms may include burning urination and a pus-like discharge from the urethra. The infection may involve only her vulva, urethra, bladder, vagina and cervix—or it can extend to her uterus, tubes and ovaries. A man who becomes infected with gonorrhea may not notice any problem for some time. When there are symptoms, early signs of trouble may include a fairly heavy, pus-like discharge from the penis.

HUMAN IMMUNODEFICIENCY VIRUS (HIV): A virus that attacks white blood cells (T-Lymphocytes) in human blood. The weakened state of the immune system allows otherwise controllable infections to result in disease.

HUMAN PAPILLOMAVIRUS (HPV): HPV can cause growths of soft warts on the genitals. In men, the warts can develop on the penis, on the scrotum, or sometimes (due to anal intercourse) in or around the anus. They can also occur in the groin area. These warts are very contagious. The human papillomavirus can cause changes in the skin cells of the penis, the vagina and the vulva that may develop into precancerous growths. HPV infections are caused by a whole group of viruses of which there are over 60 types.

SYPHILIS: A sexually transmitted disease that results from infection with the syphilis organism, Treponema pallidum. This is a spirochete, so named because of its somewhat corkscrew-shaped appearance. The syphilis organism can be transmitted only from one moist area to another and it is almost entirely a sexually transmitted disease. In the initial stage of syphilis, a chancre (which is a blister or pimple-like sore) will develop at the place where the organism invaded the body. These sores may appear on the vulva, in the vagina (or on the penis), in the mouth, or on the lips. The most typical characteristic of a syphilitic chancre is that it is painless. Secondary syphilis develops from six weeks to six months after initial infection. Symptoms may include headache, fatigue, low grade fever, skin rash and enlarged lymph nodes.

TRICHOMONIASIS: Also known as trichomonal vaginitis, it is an infection caused by a protozoan Trichomonas vaginalis. Except in rare cases, this parasite is spread only by sexual intercourse. Trichomoniasis causes a vaginal discharge and itching of the vulva. Tenderness and burning of the vulva frequently accompany the infection, often leading to pain with intercourse. Men who have contracted this infection occasionally have a discharge from the penis, but usually have no other symptoms. Very rarely, they may have occasional slight burning with urination. Trichomoniasis is now known to be one of the most common STDs in the world.

STD BADGE EXAMPLE

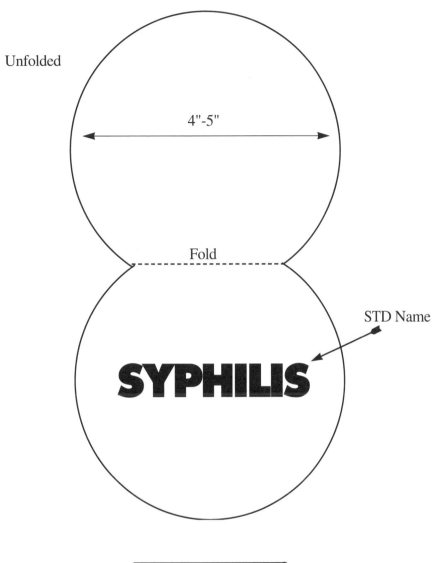

Unfolded

4"-5"

Fold

STD Name

SYPHILIS

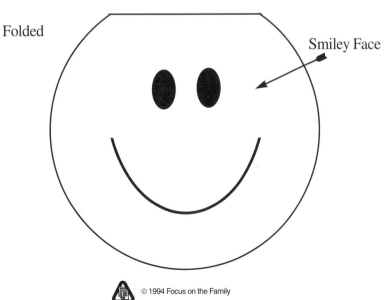

Folded

Smiley Face

4 Stop & Regain Control

Objective for teens

1. To be able to analyze the problems of a premarital sexual relationship.

2. To be able to discuss the potential for long-term emotional problems with continued premarital sexual activity.

3. To be able to understand how to regain sexual self-control (secondary virginity).

4. To be able to identify the benefits of regaining sexual self-control.

Overview

This lesson will teach teens that those who engage in risk-taking behaviors can regain self-control and begin to enjoy the benefits associated with healthy living.

Materials

• Chalkboard or flip chart
• Overhead projector
• Masking tape

Transparencies

• Benefits of Sexual Self-Control
• "Will the Real You Please Stand Up?" poem

Handouts

• Parent/teen activity handout
• Scripture reference sheet

Vocabulary

• promiscuity   • sexual self-control
• secondary virginity • virginity

Reminder: Scripture meanings can be abstract and too difficult for teens to grasp. Therefore, use the analogies and appropriate language during interpretations of scripture. Distribute the "Scripture Reference Sheets" to the group. Make sure difficult vocabulary words are defined.

INTRODUCTION

Give the group a brief overview of the lesson by reviewing the following key points:

- Committed love is worth the wait.

- Practicing or regaining sexual self-control has short- and long-term benefits.

- Success in life is often accomplished through the experience of past mistakes.

God values virginity. Virginity is a special gift that one gives to his spouse in marriage. It should be taken seriously. However, our society downgrades the state of virginity and does not recognize the value and beauty of its meaning.

Virginity is a special part of a person's sexuality. Those who remain virgins until marriage are able to focus on their intellectual, emotional, social, spiritual and moral growth. And they can develop genuine relationships without having to worry about sexual involvement.

If a person has lost his virginity, he may see no reason to stop having sex. Although he has lost his virginity *physically*, he can still decide to stop having sex and enjoy the emotional and physical benefits of waiting until marriage. For example, think of someone who has quit smoking after ten years. Although his lungs may be impaired physically, he can enjoy all the benefits of a non-smoker: his hair, clothes and breath will not smell like cigarettes, his teeth will whiten and his fingers will no longer be yellow. After awhile, he will be considered a non-smoker by both himself *and* others.

In the video, popular abstinence speaker Miles McPherson said, "Every time you have sex, you give a piece of yourself away." The physical bond loses its impact in a premarital sexual relationship because it lacks a loving marital commitment. In a marriage, a couple promises to themselves and to society that they are committed to stay together. This public declaration is different than a couple merely telling one another they are committed—it is easier to walk away from a dating relationship than a marriage.

According to the words of Christ, there are specific steps that a person needs to follow prior to marriage and these are explained in detail in Matthew 19:4-6. **"'Haven't you read,' he replied, 'that at the beginning the Creator "made them male and female,"' and said "For this reason a man will leave his father and mother and be united to his wife, and the two will become one flesh"? So they are no longer two, but one. Therefore what God has joined together, let man not separate.'"** It is only within the context of marriage that sexual union has God's blessing.

If a person has been involved in a premarital sexual relationship he can stop. He needs to find strength in God and desire His help in order to change. Paul tells us, **"For when we were controlled by the sinful nature, the sinful passions aroused by the law were at work in our bodies, so that we bore fruit for death. But now, by dying to what once bound us, we have been released from the law so that we serve in the new way of the Spirit, and not in the old way of the written code."**—(Romans 7:5,6)

ACTIVITY: STOP AND REGAIN SELF-CONTROL

TIME: 20 minutes

Use the "Benefits of Sexual Self-Control" transparency and discuss the freedoms involved with secondary virginity.

- **Free from pregnancy.** If a teenager stops having sex, he is free from being involved in an unplanned pregnancy and having to help financially support and raise a child.

- **Free from the adoption decision.** While adoption can be a positive decision, it is hard for everyone involved. The bond which may form between the parents and the unborn baby prior to adoption is difficult to break.

- **Free from the physical and emotional problems associated with abortion.** Abortion can have a lasting impact on both parents. Teens and adults alike have experienced the painful consequences of abortion.

- **Free from sexually transmitted diseases.** There is a strong relationship between the rise in teenage sexual activity and the rise in the number of teens acquiring STDs. Many STDs cannot be seen or felt and some can lead to sterility or death.

- **Free from the risks and side effects of the pill, IUD and other contraceptives.** Contraceptives are never 100 percent effective and all have some type of side effect.

- **Free from marrying someone too soon.** Often, young people may think that they have a strong relationship when it is actually grounded in physical attraction. Some couples avoid dealing with problems by engaging in sex. This leaves them knowing how to communicate only on a physical level while problems continue to mount. This usually causes the relationship to end. Practicing self-control enables one to determine whether he is in a healthy or an unhealthy relationship.

- **Free from unintentional exploitation.** Most teens are looking for intimacy, not sex. In most cases, those who end up having sex regret it later.

- **Free to know you have not damaged your (or someone else's) reproductive health.** If a teen says "yes" to sex today, he may not realize what tomorrow can bring. Many do not experience any signs or symptoms from an STD (such as chlamydia), yet it can leave them sterile. Often the problem is discovered too late.

- **Free to pursue life goals.** Remind the group of the activity "My Future Matters" in lesson three. A teen who says "no" to sex today will be able to concentrate on reaching his goals and fulfilling his dreams.

- **Free to respect yourself and others.** Self-esteem is earned and learned. When a young person controls his sexual desires, he builds his self-esteem and develops a respect for his body.

- **Free to establish a greater trust in marriage.** The practice of self-control creates discipline. Good marriages take work, patience and trust—the same components of self-control.

- **Free to enjoy being a teenager without pressure.** It is hard enough to be a teenager without the physical and emotional problems associated with sexual relationships.

ACTIVITY:
HEALTHY BEHAVIORS AND MARRIAGE

TIME: 15 minutes

So often, individuals think that once they marry, their spouse's unhealthy habits will magically disappear. Unfortunately, what most engaged people fail to realize is that, most likely, their future spouse has been practicing those behaviors for years. Habits are easily acquired but can take years to overcome. For instance, a young woman may think that once she marries her boyfriend, he will stop smoking or drinking or staying out with his friends until all hours. It is unrealistic to think that his behavior will change once he has a ring on his finger.

Teenagers who smoke, drink or engage in premarital sex may have a hard time putting a stop to their unhealthy behaviors in the future. And, these habits can adversely affect not only their own futures, but their spouse's and children's as well.

Use the following questions to stimulate group discussion:

What types of healthy behaviors can contribute to a good marriage?
Responses may include: hard work, good communication, honesty and trustworthiness. Write responses on the board. Circle the characteristics that they can be working on right now in order to contribute to a healthy marriage. For instance, point out the fact that *communication, compatibility, unconditional love* and *commitment* are four essential elements of a successful marriage.

How can you practice being a good communicator?
Responses may include: as a member of my youth group, as a student in the classroom, as a brother or sister at home, or with friends.

How can you practice being compatible?
Responses may include: being a good listener, trying to understand another's point of view, and celebrating someone else's good news.

How can you practice unconditional love?
Responses may include: helping Mom do the laundry, cheering up a friend when he is feeling down, and helping Dad mow the lawn when you don't feel like it.

How can you practice commitment?
Responses may include: being on time for class, turning in assignments on time, and following instructions from the coach.

ACTIVITY: MOVING WITH THE CROWD

TIME: 5 minutes

Use the "Will the Real You Please Stand Up?" transparency and select a teen to read the poem. Ask the group to respond to the following question: "What does the title of the poem mean?" Most likely, responses will widely vary.

Reread the line in the poem that states, "When 40 million people believe in a dumb idea, it's still a dumb idea." Stress that if "40 million" teenagers engage in premarital sex, it *still* doesn't make it a good idea. The emotional and physical consequences still exist. At one point in time, thousands of people thought slavery and Hitler's plans were beneficial. But owning slaves and killing Jews caused great suffering. In the course of history, it took two major wars to fight for what was right.

It is important for teens to associate with those who are responsible, courageous and who can practice self-control. Friends can help one another achieve goals, strive for excellence and maintain their moral standards.

Friends can help or hinder a young person's struggle to handle peer pressure. The kind of television shows or lyrics they listen to can influence their behavior in a positive or negative way. Media messages have been shaping our culture for several decades. And, more than ever, teenagers are being bombarded with distorted messages regarding human sexuality.

Sexual messages are sent daily through the television, movies, music and print advertising. MTV provides plenty of music videos showing couples in various stages of physical intimacy. Soap operas target many of their stories toward teen issues and count on their sexual scenes to draw viewers. Soaps, music videos and advertising often are not based on reality. We rarely see the outcome of the pictured fantasies. Pose the following question: "When do promiscuous soap opera characters visit a local health clinic to be treated for genital warts, herpes or syphilis?" Remind teens of the need to differentiate between reality and fantasy while at the movies, watching television or listening to the radio.

CONCLUSION

Those who practice sexual self-control will reap short- and long-term benefits. It is a positive and healthy habit that can lead to great marital fulfillment. Remind teens that **the best defense *is* a good offense**. Setting guidelines and standards can help them reach their goals and realize their dreams.

Distribute the scripture reference sheet and the parent/teen activity handout. Request that the activity handout is completed prior to next meeting.

SCRIPTURE REFERENCE SHEET

"'Haven't you read,' he replied, 'that at the beginning the Creator "made them male and female," and said, "For this reason a man will leave his father and mother and be united to his wife, and the two will become one flesh"? So they are no longer two, but one. Therefore what God has joined together, let man not separate.'" Matthew 19:4-6

"For when we were controlled by the sinful nature, the sinful passions aroused by the law were at work in our bodies, so that we bore fruit for death. But now, by dying to what once bound us, we have been released by the law so that we serve in the new way of the Spirit, and not in the old way of the written code." Romans 7:5,6

OVERVIEW

This lesson taught teens that it is possible for those who engage in risk-taking behavior to regain self-control and begin enjoying the benefits associated with healthy living.

SCRIPTURE OBJECTIVE

Teens will be able to identify the fruits of God's forgiveness.

PARENT/TEEN DISCUSSION ACTIVITY

1. Parent:
   Discuss how you have learned from your past mistakes.

2. Parent and teen:
   Discuss the benefits of practicing or regaining sexual self-control. How would this also apply to dieting, drinking or smoking?

WILL THE REAL YOU PLEASE STAND UP?

Submit to
pressure
from peers
and you move
down to their
level.
Speak up
for your own
beliefs
and you invite
them up to your
level.
If you move
with the crowd,
you'll get
no further than
the crowd.
When 40 million
people believe in
a dumb idea,
it's still a
dumb idea.
Simply swimming
with the tide
leaves you
nowhere.
So if you believe in
something
that's good,
honest and bright—
stand up for it.
Maybe your peers
will get smart
and drift
your way.

United Technologies Corporation, Hartford, CT 06141 as published in *The Wall Street Journal*.

BENEFITS OF SEXUAL SELF-CONTROL

• Free from pregnancy.

• Free from the adoption decision.

• Free from the physical and emotional problems associated with an abortion.

• Free from sexually transmitted diseases.

• Free from the risks and side effects of the pill, IUD and other contraceptives.

• Free from marrying someone too soon.

• Free from unintentional exploitation.

• Free to know you have not damaged your (or someone else's) reproductive health.

• Free to pursue life goals.

• Free to respect yourself and others.

• Free to establish a greater trust in your marriage.

• Free to enjoy being a teenager without pressure.

HIV/AIDS in Today's Society

INTRODUCTION

Sex, Lies and . . . the Truth presents a clear, twofold message regarding teen sexuality. One message focuses on the risks and consequences, both physical and emotional, of adolescent sex. The video contains a recurring theme of a carnival midway, lined with barkers and hucksters attempting to lure passersby into rigged games of chance—as a symbol for the many voices which entice teenagers into risky sexual experiences. Sex is not a game of chance, or a game at all. The video strives to help teens build a solid understanding of the importance of the future as opposed to engaging in sex for temporary pleasure.

The second message emphasizes the benefits of waiting for sex. Kirk Cameron and Chelsea Noble present a positive view of sexuality within the context of a permanent, committed and exclusive relationship. Their comments about the enjoyment of truly safe sex sharply contrast with the fear, pain and despair which are so commonly experienced in the wake of adolescent sexual encounters.

UTILIZING THE VIDEO

The purpose of *Sex, Lies and . . . the Truth* is to promote the value of abstinence in the context of the current epidemic of crisis pregnancies, sexually transmitted diseases and HIV/AIDS. Postponing sex until marriage is presented as a wise decision, one that is not only endorsed by credible role-models, but is in fact more common among teens than they might realize. (Despite their seemingly endless talk about sex, national surveys continue to indicate that the majority of adolescents are *not* sexually active.[1])

Much of this video takes the form of comments and opinions about sex from a wide variety of sources, expressing ideas which run the gamut from articulate insight to woeful ignorance. One skill which teens can hone while watching this material is that of becoming critical viewers—a capability they need as they are repeatedly exposed to sexual content in films, music, TV programs and commercials. They should be encouraged to identify both the truth and the fantasy in many of the statements made during the video.

From time to time, it may be appropriate to stop the tape and ask an open-ended question, such as "What do you think of what he/she just said?" or "If someone said that to you, how would you respond?" This may stimulate both vigorous discussion and vital learning.

Not only is the discussion of HIV/AIDS emotionally charged, it is also politically charged. Medical experts first told us about "safe sex," and when that didn't prove true, it was changed to "safer sex." The definitions continue to change as the political winds change. The definition of abstinence has also been immersed in a political correctness battle. There have been references to "periodic abstinence" or "abstinence practiced consistently and correctly." These references are merely another term for periodic sexual activity, not abstinence! The definition of **abstinence** for the purpose of this study guide is **refraining from all sexual activity, which includes intercourse, oral sex, anal sex, mutual masturbation, etc.; the only 100 percent effective means of preventing pregnancy and the spread of sexually transmitted diseases.**

Objectives for teens:

1. To understand the basic meaning of the acronyms HIV and AIDS.
2. To learn how HIV is transmitted.
3. To debunk myths and misunderstandings about transmission of HIV.
4. To realize that all sexually active people—especially teenagers—can be HIV infected.
5. To acknowledge one's own risk for infection if participating in high risk activities—that is, to individualize and personalize this issue.
6. To recognize that this disease is worth avoiding, and that each person (with very rare exception) makes the choices which determine whether or not he becomes infected.
7. To be motivated to make the choices necessary to avoid HIV infection.
8. To understand the role any individual can play in befriending those who are infected and help them cope with their disease.

[Note: It will take more than just showing teens this video to accomplish these objectives.]

Overview

This lesson will present basic information about HIV and motivate teens to value their lives enough to choose behaviors which will prevent them from becoming infected with HIV. This includes learning how HIV is (and is not) transmitted, the impact of this disease on individuals and their families, avoidance of infection and encouragement to stop high-risk activities. In addition, teens are motivated to view those already infected with HIV as people with whom they can safely build friendships.

Materials

• *Sex, Lies and . . . the Truth* video

Transparencies

• Modes of HIV transmission
• Myths of contracting HIV
• "Complete the Sentence"

Handouts

• Parent/teen handout
• HIV take-home assignment

Vocabulary

• abstinence	• herpes simplex II	• marriage	• sexually transmitted
• AIDS	• HIV	• monogamous	disease (STD)
• candida albicans	• HIV positive	• pneumonia	• tuberculosis
• cervix	• immune system	• psychosis	• urethra
• dementia	• IV (intravenous)	• retrovirus	• uterus
• ectropion	• lymphocyte		

LESSON TOPICS

1. Definitions of HIV and AIDS.

2. Understanding universal risk.

3. Impact of HIV on the infected individual (physical and emotional).

4. Modes of HIV transmission.

5. Myths of HIV transmission:

    a. HIV can be spread through casual, everyday contact.

    b. HIV can be spread by mosquitoes and other biting insects.

    c. HIV can be spread by a casual kiss.

    d. If I am exclusively heterosexual, I don't need to worry about HIV/AIDS.

    e. If I am not in a high risk group, I don't need to worry about HIV/AIDS.

    f. By engaging in "safe sex," I can eliminate any risk of contracting HIV.

    g. Using spermicides containing Nonoxynol-9, along with a condom, makes sex less risky.

6. Testing of HIV:

    a. Why be tested?

    b. Who should be tested?

    c. Where should testing be done?

7. Overcoming discrimination against infected people.

8. Avoiding HIV infection.

9. Building decision-making, negotiation and refusal skills.

1. DEFINITIONS OF HIV AND AIDS

HIV/AIDS is an infection caused by the Human Immunodeficiency Virus (HIV), a member of a group called retroviruses, which are known to survive for a very prolonged time period between initial contact and the onset of symptoms. HIV may produce a brief flu-like illness at first, after which no symptoms may be noted for several years. During this time, however, the virus multiplies within a certain subgroup of lymphocytes (a form of white blood cells) and eventually destroys them. This ultimately leaves the infected person unable to fight off a wide variety of organisms, including other viruses (i.e. herpes simplex), fungi (i.e. the common cause of yeast infections: candida albicans), bacteria (i.e. tuberculosis) and parasites. An infected person is also prone to develop certain types of cancer, such as Kaposi's sarcoma (a cancer affecting skin that was rare in young adults until the AIDS epidemic) or lymphoma. The virus also directly damages the central nervous system and may produce a variety of syndromes, especially dementia—the loss of intellectual function. Overall, this phase of the illness is referred to as the Acquired Immune Deficiency Syndrome, or AIDS.

2. UNDERSTANDING UNIVERSAL RISK

Everyone is at risk of infection if, and *only if,* they are involved in high risk activities. This virus does not discriminate on the basis of gender, race, economic status, where you live or any other factors. Those who engage in high risk activities are putting themselves in danger of contracting HIV. Those who don't, aren't. It is that simple. Teens need to know that the choice is theirs. No one is immune to HIV.

It is also important to remember that, in this context, most of those infected are unaware of the presence of the virus in their bodies. Thus, they do not know enough to protect the people they honestly care about and love from infection. It is never safe to assume that a potential sexual or needle-sharing partner is not infected. Of course, the more partners one has, the greater the risk of infection. However, there are many who have been infected through their first encounter with sex or needles.

3. IMPACT OF HIV ON THE INFECTED INDIVIDUAL

Physical: While there are reports of people infected with HIV dying in as little as seven months,[2] it can take up to ten years for some of those infected to progress to the point of diagnosis with AIDS. During this time, the virus is actively multiplying in the body with incredible numbers of viruses concentrating in the lymph nodes.[3]

After the initial flu-like episode (if any), the HIV-infected person typically lives for months or years without any signs of illness at all. Unfortunately, it is possible for the individual to transmit the virus to others during this prolonged period while he or she feels well. Eventually, symptoms such as fever, sweats, enlarged lymph nodes, diarrhea and fatigue develop and persist, at which time the diagnosis of HIV infection is usually made (if it was not previously known). At this time, it is assumed that all people with HIV will eventually develop full-blown AIDS and die from its consequences—although medical intervention may delay the process.

Once the immune system is seriously compromised, the individual develops increasingly severe and disabling illnesses. Pneumonia (infection of lung tissue) with unusual organisms is very common. Debilitating fatigue, marked weight loss and constant diarrhea typically occur. Central nervous system disturbances, including seizures, psychosis or loss of intellectual function may seriously compromise the person's ability to cope and function. Complex medical care is usually necessary to help combat the various infections or to provide palliation (comfort measures) during the late stages of the disease.

Emotional: In addition to the physical impact, people infected with HIV suffer many of the same emotional and psychological problems as those with other chronic or terminal illnesses. These can include depression (including suicidal tendencies), loneliness, fear and a sense of lost control of their lives. They may also have to deal with rejection by family and friends and loss of employment, insurance and even housing. Medical treatment for HIV infection—especially when it has progressed to AIDS—can be very expensive, adding further to the overall sense of devastation. People infected with HIV need friends who are not afraid to spend time with them, understand that their lives are important, and will help them focus their attention on life and living with AIDS rather than dying of AIDS.

4. MODES OF HIV TRANSMISSION

From the earliest days after the virus is transmitted, all who become infected with HIV can, in turn, transmit the virus to others, though not through casual contact. With the exception of rare cases in which mothers have infected their babies through breast feeding, there are only three body fluids with a sufficient concentration of virus to transmit it. These are blood, male sexual fluid (including pre-ejaculatory fluid[4]) and female sexual fluid. Any activity that can introduce any one of these fluids from an infected person into the blood stream or into contact with a mucous membrane (i.e. eyes, nose, mouth, urethra, vagina or anus) of another can result in infection.

Sex: HIV can be sexually transmitted to either partner, whether in a heterosexual or homosexual relationship. Worldwide, at least 75 percent of all cases have been transmitted heterosexually.[5] The virus may be transmitted during vaginal, oral or anal sex, with anal receptive intercourse being particularly risky because of the likelihood of physical trauma. Risk of transmission also increases with the number of contacts with an infected partner *and* the number of partners overall. However, it should be stressed that HIV infection can follow a single contact, and the apparent health of a partner has no bearing on the possibility of transmission.

No one can tell merely by appearance whether a person is infected. All who are infected are able to infect others. Lack of symptoms does not mean that a person is not infectious. Many who are infected are unaware. Some people who do know they are HIV positive will not reveal their status so they can have sex. Thus, **any sex—other than in a permanent, mutually faithful relationship with a partner known to be uninfected—is dangerous.**

Blood and Blood Products: Transmission of HIV through transfusion with contaminated blood products has been extremely uncommon since 1985, when all United States blood banks began using a sensitive test to detect HIV infection in all potential donors.[6] Therefore, the major source of blood transmission of HIV today is shared needles.[7] While most of these cases involve injecting street drugs, athletes sharing needles to shoot steroids are also at risk. For that matter, young people sharing needles for anything (i.e., ear piercing, home tattoos, blood brother/sister rituals) can become infected if one of the individuals is infected with HIV.

Mothers to Newborns: Some 25 to 30 percent of babies born to infected mothers are infected with HIV.[8, 9, 10] Unfortunately, most die before their fifth birthday. Virtually all newborns whose mothers are infected with HIV test positive at birth because the mother's antibody to the virus is present in the infant's blood. (The same phenomenon occurs with measles, rubella and other viral infections to which the mother has been exposed in the past.) Those babies not infected at birth lose the HIV antibody between 9 and 18 months of age, and further testing can demonstrate that they are not infected. As noted above, transmission from mother to child via breast milk has been reported.

5. MYTHS OF HIV TRANSMISSION

A. "HIV can be spread through casual, everyday contact."

There is strong evidence that HIV is not spread through normal social (non-sexual) contact. This includes spending time in the same room, hugging, holding hands or using the same toilet seat. A number of studies of people who lived in the same home with infected persons have found that, other than sexual or needle-sharing partners, no one has become infected after years of close contact.[11, 12]

Body fluids, other than blood and sexual fluids, do not have enough virus in them to infect. Thus, there is no need for concern about contact with tears, saliva, perspiration, urine, etc. The only exception is when blood is in one of these fluids, as might be the case in deep kissing, or when there is a significant amount of the virus, which is characteristic in the early and late stages of the disease.

B. "HIV can be spread by mosquitoes and other biting insects."

Mosquitoes and other blood-sucking insects do not spread HIV. HIV does not survive in the body of insects in sufficient quantity to be secreted through saliva to initiate an infection.

C. "HIV can be spread by a kiss."

Typically, there is far too little concentration of HIV in the saliva of an infected person for transmission to occur through kissing.[13] However, several factors can increase HIV concentration in saliva to cause concern. These include the final stage of the disease and the presence of blood in the saliva. Brushing or flossing teeth, eating crunchy foods, sores in the mouth and a number of other circumstances may introduce blood into saliva. In such situations, transmission could occur during deep or passionate kissing with an infected individual—especially if the kissing results in a tongue being cut on a sharp tooth or braces. Thus, while kissing an HIV-infected individual is relatively safe, deep or passionate kissing poses some risk.

D. "If I am exclusively heterosexual, I don't need to worry about HIV/AIDS."

It may seem strange to see this under the heading of "myths," but myths persist that if you are heterosexual you need not worry about HIV, that only women can be infected heterosexually, etc. The virus is spread efficiently both from male to female and female to male during vaginal intercourse.[14] At least 75 percent of the world's AIDS cases have been transmitted heterosexually. In parts of the world with almost exclusive heterosexual spread, the ratio of infected women to men is virtually equal.[15, 16]

E. "If I am not in a high risk group, I don't need to worry about HIV/AIDS."

One of the most dangerous myths to arise in HIV/AIDS education has been that of high-risk groups. Risk relates to activities far more than to groups. Because of the high risk group concept, people have become infected believing they were not at risk.[17, 18] It is tempting, upon hearing a list of "risk groups" to say, "Well, I'm not that, and I'm not that . . . I guess I don't need to worry about this disease." However, HIV does not care about group identification. If we do things that put us at risk, then we *are* at risk.

F. "By engaging in "safe sex," I can eliminate any risk of contracting HIV."

The *only* safe sex is between uninfected partners in a permanent, mutually exclusive relationship, as in marriage. **Period.**

If the HIV status of a partner is not known with *absolute certainty*, sexual contact with him is a potentially life-threatening activity. A clean cut appearance, apparent good health and a relatively uneventful sexual history *aren't guarantees of safety*. Unfortunately, not everyone is willing to be forthright about past sexual contacts, and even complete honesty cannot account for all of the possible effects of those experiences. As former Surgeon General C. Everett Koop has pointed out, when you have sex with a particular partner, you are also, in effect, having sex with all of that person's previous partners, and all of those partners' partners, and so on.

Furthermore, more than two-thirds of infected people are unaware of their HIV status [19], and some who *do* know that they are infected may not reveal this fact to a potential partner. And, HIV is not the only important sexually transmitted disease (STD). A person who is not infected with HIV can transmit any of several other organisms, many of which can cause serious disease or even death.

Safe sex is only found within a mutually faithful, monogamous relationship (i.e. marriage) wherein both partners are uninfected.

G. "Using spermicides containing Nonoxynol-9 along with a condom makes sex less risky."

For years, people have been told that the use of spermicides containing Nonoxynol-9, along with a condom, can make sex with a potentially infected partner even less dangerous. This chemical has been shown in laboratory testing to be capable of killing HIV. However, one recent study with prostitutes, half who used Nonoxynol-9 and half who did not, found that those using Nonoxynol-9 had a higher infection rate than those who did not.[20] The chemical can cause irritation of the vaginal walls, which increases concentration of white blood cells—the target of HIV—in the vaginal mucosa.

6. TESTING FOR HIV

HIV antibody testing is one of the strategies being used to slow the spread of this epidemic.

A. Why be tested?

Most people who have been involved in high risk activities experience fear of infection. Those who are infected need that knowledge as early as possible so that they can seek treatment to keep them healthy for as long as possible. They also need to know the risk they pose to sexual and needle-sharing partners so that they can be sure to avoid infecting them. For this same reason, at-risk women and their partners should be tested prior to child-bearing.

B. Who should be tested?

All who have participated in high risk activities (exchange of bodily fluids through sexual activity or needle-sharing) should be tested. Those who have not participated in high risk activities may want to be tested to be sure of their HIV status. It is a good idea for both partners to have tests prior to marriage.

C. Where should testing be done?

The HIV antibody test requires a simple blood draw, which can be carried out in a private physician's office, clinic or health department. In most states, local health departments and other testing sites offer free or low-cost screening, accompanied by counseling. In order to preserve confidentiality, consent must be obtained prior to the blood being drawn. In addition, most states have strict laws regarding the handling of results, also to protect confidentiality.

Blood donated at a hospital or blood bank is always tested for HIV antibodies, and these facilities will notify donors if the test is positive. However, individuals should *not* donate blood as an indirect method of checking HIV status. Most facilities will readily direct a caller to testing sites in the community.

7. OVERCOMING DISCRIMINATION AGAINST HIV-INFECTED PEOPLE

Discrimination is not merely an issue of civil rights or even basic compassion. It is also a key element in slowing the spread of HIV. Until we understand that HIV infection can happen to anyone who is involved in high-risk activities, we will not take those risks seriously or be motivated to avoid them. In addition, fear of discrimination continues to prevent many from being tested for HIV or other appropriate health care.

Inappropriate fears built on myths about modes of transmission need to be dispelled. As noted previously, people with HIV/AIDS need friends just as much as anyone else, and they should never be subject to any form of harassment or ridicule.

8. AVOIDING HIV INFECTION

A. Sexual contact

For the past decade, the concept of "safe sex" or "safer sex" practices have been promoted as a method of reducing the transmission of HIV. These include:

- Limiting the number of sexual partners an individual has.

- Inquiring about a potential partner's past sexual experiences and HIV status.

- Avoiding practices, such as anal receptive intercourse, in which tissue damage and exposure to blood are likely to occur.

- Understanding that condom use is risk *reduction,* **not** a risk *elimination* method.

Undoubtedly, if followed, these practices reduce the likelihood of acquiring HIV during sex—but calling such sex "safe" is certainly optimistic.

- Some have adopted the practice of "serial monogamy"—having one sexual partner at a time—as a way of limiting potential exposure to HIV and other sexually transmitted diseases. But, as noted previously, each successive partner carries into the relationship the fallout from all prior contacts and those contacts' contacts, and so on. Furthermore, only one sexual encounter can start an HIV infection (or, for that matter, any number of several other STDs).

- Determining the extent of a potential partner's sexual history is an awkward exercise at best, and one which may be forgotten during the heat of the moment. Furthermore, selective memory—or outright deception— may occur when one partner is eagerly anticipating a sexual experience.

- While avoidance of physically traumatizing sex is obviously wise, HIV is perfectly capable of being transmitted during *any* sexual encounter.

- Latex condoms have been the most widely promoted component of "safer sex." But their effectiveness has been frequently overstated.

A 1992 study in *Family Planning Perspectives* found an overall rate of condom malfunctioning—through breakage or slipping off the penis during intercourse or withdrawal—of nearly 15 percent.[21]

When condoms alone are used for birth control, the failure rate for preventing pregnancy has long been conservatively estimated to be 10 to 15 percent. That is, out of 100 sexually active women, 10 to 15 will be pregnant within one year. But while conception can only occur during a short window of time (two or three days out of a month), HIV may be transmitted *every* day of the month. And while sperm must travel some distance from the vagina to a woman's fallopian tubes for conception to occur, HIV does not have to travel from the point of contact to begin an infection.

Not surprisingly, a more recent analysis of several studies of HIV transmission among married couples, in which one member is HIV positive, suggested an overall condom failure rate of 31 percent for preventing HIV transmission.[22] This rate of potential exposure to a lethal disease is one that few would consider safe. (Indeed, no work site, recreational activity or form of public transportation would be allowed to operate with even a 10 percent risk of a serious mishap to its participants over a 12 month period.)

Truly safe sex can only be enjoyed by persons who postpone sexual activity until they have committed themselves to a permanent, monogamous, and mutually faithful relationship (as in marriage). Of course, their partner must be free of infection. Anything short of that, whether or not condoms are used, cannot realistically be considered safe.

B. Contact with blood

As noted above, the risk of HIV infection through blood transfusion has been virtually eliminated.[23] Nevertheless, those who know they will be undergoing major surgery in the future often can arrange for "directed donations" from people they know to be disease-free (although all donations are tested anyway). Or, they may be able to donate and store some of their own blood for use after surgery, if needed. This is called an "autologous transfusion."[24]

The most common means of transmission of contaminated blood now is through needles and syringes shared by IV drug users. The drug itself does not carry the virus, but blood left behind from the previous user(s) may be injected into the next user. *No needles or other instruments which pierce the skin should be shared.* Other accidental blood contact should also be avoided as much as possible. If, for example, someone has a bloody nose, that person should be handed tissue to use, and it is best for others not to touch the blood, if at all possible. (In medical offices and hospitals, personnel are taught "universal precautions" which assume that *anyone's* blood might be contaminated.)

C. Drug use

Aside from the risks of using IV drugs, other "recreational" drugs—especially alcohol—impair judgment and decision-making abilities. Unintended sexual contact and other risky behavior are far more likely to occur while "under the influence." One study found that, when questioned, a majority of sexually active college teens reported at least one unwanted sexual experience while under the influence of alcohol or other drugs.[25]

D. Babies

Obviously, avoiding HIV infection in the first place is the most certain way for a woman to prevent an infection in her child. But if a pregnant woman is in fact HIV positive, there is still a 70 to 75 percent likelihood that her baby will *not* be infected.[26,27,28]

As noted earlier, HIV-infected mothers should not nurse their infants because of the small risk of transmission through breast milk.

9. BUILDING DECISION-MAKING, NEGOTIATION AND REFUSAL SKILLS

Most teens are smart enough to make good decisions and strong enough to carry them out when they are given adequate information and are equipped with the skills to put those decisions into action.

When they are given opportunities to make decisions, even little ones, teens learn the skills of processing information, prioritizing values and balancing consequences. The latter is a vital concept. They must learn from experience that decisions have consequences.

Once they decide not to use drugs, to wait for sex, or to take other steps to avoid infection, there are a number of ways to equip young people to stick with those decisions. It is important for adults to know that young people *are* looking for ways to say "no" without losing a friend or hurting the other person's feelings.[29] Many, if faced with a choice between carrying out their decision to wait for sex or losing a friendship, will choose friendship and take the risk. Some 73 percent of sexually active girls and 50 percent of boys report that the primary motivation for their first sexual experience was peer pressure.[30]

Teens need to be trained to resist pressure in ways that will not terminate friendships. Role playing can help them think through scenarios that might involve risk and consider acceptable responses.

Another effective tool is to encourage the development of friendships with teens who share their values. It has been wisely said, "Show me your friends and I'll show you your future." When in a group where the adoption of risk-free behaviors is the accepted norm, there is strong positive pressure from peers.[31] Some churches have established groups for teens who have committed to wait until marriage to have sex.

Others provide wallet cards teens can sign and display proclaiming their decision to wait. These can help teens make their decision clear to their friends from the beginning so that it will come as no surprise when they decline to participate in risky activities. While this can produce some initial taunting, it also often results in decreased pressure to become involved.

ACTIVITY: HIV/AIDS CONCERNS US ALL

TIME: 25 minutes

Break the group into teams of approximately six teens each. Have the teams take approximately 10 minutes to compose a letter to the editor of a local newspaper about an HIV/AIDS related topic (sex in advertising, countering myths, befriending people with HIV, need for more HIV testing facilities, encouraging people at risk to be tested, etc.).

Have each team leader share the composed letter and have a panel of judges pick their favorite letter. Give the winning group a prize.

ACTIVITY: COMPLETE THE SENTENCE

TIME: 20 minutes

Use the "Complete the Sentence" transparency. Have the group contribute various responses to the sentences listed. After teens suggest answers, discuss the response, such as "Fearing HIV is . . . "

ACTIVITY: HELPING PEOPLE AND FAMILIES WITH HIV

TIME: 30-40 minutes

Break the group into teams of approximately six people each. Ask the questions: "If you had three hours a week to donate to helping HIV-infected individuals, what would you do for them?" and "What would you consider doing for their families?"

TAKE-HOME ASSIGNMENT

1. Describe ways to befriend and help a person infected with HIV.

2. Describe three ways a person can contract the HIV virus. Describe three myths about contracting the HIV virus.

3. Your friend comes to you and says he thinks he has been exposed to the HIV virus through a risky activity. What advice would you give to your friend?

PARENT/TEEN ACTIVITY HANDOUT

Discuss the following questions with one or both of your parents:

1. If one of our family members contracted HIV, what would we do? How would we help? What services would we try to find for the infected member of the family?

2. Do you (parent) know the primary ways HIV is transmitted? Do you know what some of the myths are regarding how you can contract HIV?

3. Why is it a good idea to test for HIV if you have been involved in high risk activities?

MODES OF HIV TRANSMISSION

- **SEX**

- **BLOOD**

- **MOTHERS TO BABIES**

MYTHS OF CONTRACTING HIV

1. HIV can be spread through casual, everyday contact.

2. HIV can be spread by mosquitoes and other biting insects.

3. HIV can be spread by casual kissing.

4. If I am exclusively heterosexual, I don't need to worry about HIV/AIDS.

5. If I am not in a high risk group, I don't need to worry about HIV/AIDS.

6. By engaging in "safe sex," I can eliminate any risk of contracting HIV.

7. Using spermicides containing Nonoxynol-9, along with a condom, makes sex less risky.

COMPLETE THE SENTENCE

AIDS is . . .

Avoiding HIV infection by waiting until marriage to have sex is . . .

Condoms are . . .

If someone in my group was infected with HIV, I would . . .

If I was infected with HIV, I would want people to . . .

The level of risk of HIV for teens is . . .

The information we are getting about HIV is . . .

If my friend becomes infected, I will . . .

VOCABULARY

ABSTINENCE Refraining from all sexual activity, which includes intercourse, oral sex, anal sex, mutual masturbation, etc.; the only 100 percent effective means of preventing pregnancy and the spread of sexually transmitted diseases; sexual self-control.

ACQUIRED IMMUNODEFICIENCY SYNDROME (AIDS) An immune-system disease, caused by a virus, in which the resistance of the body to certain infections and cancers is lowered. The virus is spread through blood, semen and other body fluids.

ADULTERY Sexual intercourse between two people, at least one of whom is married to someone else.

ANTIBODY Any of various proteins in the blood that are generated to neutralize foreign proteins and therefore produce immunity against certain microorganisms or their toxins.

ASYMPTOMATIC A person may have an STD without seeing or feeling the symptoms.

BONDING A uniting or binding element or force, as in sexual intercourse; something that binds or restrains.

CANDIDA ALBICANS A species of yeast-like fungus that can cause a variety of human infections. Common examples are diaper rashes in infants and vaginal infections in women. In AIDS patients, candida causes far more severe infections, especially in the throat and esophagus.

CERVIX The opening of the uterus into the vagina.

CHLAMYDIA An infection caused by the most common sexually transmitted microorganism in the United States. Contracted only by intercourse, its primary site of infection is a woman's cervix, tubes and ovaries. This can cause sterility and/or abdominal pain. A woman can receive the infectious organism chlamydia trachomatis from a man during intercourse and carry it in her reproductive organs. An infected woman may experience urethral discharge, burning with urination, an urgency or frequency of urination and pain in the lower abdomen just above the pubic bone.

CONDOM A sheath commonly of rubber worn over the penis during sexual intercourse intended to prevent conception or venereal infection.

DEMENTIA A condition of permanent loss of vital cognitive functions such as memory, orientation, attention, ability and judgement.

DESENSITIZE To lessen the sensitivity of; to make indifferent, unaware, or the like, in feeling.

ECTROPION The fragile lining which usually covers much of the cervix until a woman reaches her 20s or bears her first child. This lining is more easily invaded by organisms which cause sexually transmitted diseases.

EXPLOIT, EXPLOITATION To make selfish use of someone or something for one's own advantage or profit. Selfish or unfair utilization.

FORNICATION An inclusive term referring to all kinds of sexual immorality, including sexual intercourse between two unmarried people.

GENITAL HERPES The infective virus, herpes simplex type II, is spread by direct contact with someone carrying the virus. This contact may be sexual intercourse, but the virus can be spread by mouth, so herpes sores on the lips may result from kissing or from oral-genital contact with an infected individual. The common fever blister, or "cold sore," is caused by the virus herpes simplex type I. Once the herpes virus gets into the tissues, it is there to stay. An outbreak of herpes can cause enlarged lymph nodes in the groin. Flu-like symptoms may occur in the form of fever and muscle aches. In men, blisters may appear on the penis, the scrotum, or the anus; in women, the sores may be on the vulva, inside the vagina, on the cervix, or in the anal region.

GONORRHEA A contagious inflammation of the genital membranes transmitted chiefly by sexual intercourse which may involve the lower or upper genital tract, especially the uterine tubes, or spread throughout the abdomen and other structures by the bloodstream.

HERPES SIMPLEX II Herpes is caused by a virus that produces blisters and sores in and on the sex organs. The infective virus herpes simplex type II is spread by direct contact with someone who carries it. This contact may be sexual intercourse, but the virus can be spread by mouth, so herpes sores on the lips may result from kissing or from oral-genital contact with an infected individual. Herpes simplex II should be distinguished from herpes simplex I which is the virus that causes common cold sores or fever blisters.

HUMAN IMMUNODEFICIENCY VIRUS (HIV) A virus that attacks and kills off the concentration of white blood cells called T-cells. This weakened state of the immune system allows otherwise controllable infections to result in disease.

HIV POSITIVE The term which indicates that a person's blood contains antibodies to the HIV virus, indicating that he or she has been infected. A person can test positive for HIV and have no symptoms for years, but can transmit the virus to others during that time.

HUMAN PAPILLOMAVIRUS (HPV) HPV can cause growths of soft warts on the genitals. In men, the warts can develop on the penis, on the scrotum, or sometimes (due to anal intercourse) in or around the anus. They can also occur in the groin area. These warts are very contagious. The human papillomavirus can cause changes in the skin cells of the penis, the vagina and the vulva that may develop into precancerous growths. HPV infections are caused by a whole group of viruses of which there are over 60 types.

HUMAN SEXUALITY Everything that makes a person masculine or feminine, including intellectual, emotional, social, spiritual, moral and physical parts of our personhood as well as sex, sexual intercourse and body parts. The process in which we grow and develop as human beings.

IMMEDIATE GRATIFICATION Instant source of satisfaction or pleasure.

IMMUNE SYSTEM The complex network of cells and biochemical functions which serves to defend the body against invasion by organisms (i.e. viruses, bacteria, fungi and parasites).

INFATUATION Foolish or irrational love or desire.

IV (INTRAVENOUS) Injected directly into the bloodstream through a vein (as opposed to taken by mouth, or injected under skin or into muscle).

LOVE The profound, tender affection for another characterized by giving for the good of the other person, wanting what is best for that person.

LUST A passionate sexual desire or appetite.

LYMPHOCYTE A particular type of white blood cell which is important in defending the body against certain infections, especially viruses. A specific subgroup of lymphocytes is disabled and destroyed by the HIV virus.

MARRIAGE The social institution under which a man and a woman establish their decision to live as husband and wife by legal commitments, religious ceremonies, etc., for the purpose of founding and maintaining a family.

MEDIA The means of communication, as radio and television, newspapers, magazines, etc., that reach very large numbers of people.

MONOGAMOUS The practice of marrying only once during a lifetime; the state or custom of being married to one person at a time.

MORAL Pertaining to or dealing with morals or the principles of morality. Pertaining to the right and wrong in conduct.

PETTING/PHYSICAL INTIMACY Amorous fondling or caresses which are sexually stimulating. A natural stage in the progression of sexual intimacy leading to sexual intercourse.

PNEUMONIA An infection involving the lungs. Pneumonia involving a variety of organisms are common in people with AIDS.

PROMISCUITY Indiscriminate mingling or association, especially having sexual relations with a number of partners on an informal or casual basis.

PSYCHOSIS Serious mental derangement characterized by defective or lost contact with reality.

REFUSAL SKILLS To show or express unwillingness to do or comply with; to deny, give up or renounce; to withhold acceptance, compliance or permission.

RETROVIRUS A family of viruses (of which HIV is a member) known for producing symptoms months or years *after* the initial infection.

SAFE SEX Sexual activity free from harm or risk.

SECONDARY VIRGINITY A concept whereas an individual, who is no longer a virgin, practices sexual self-control as if he were a virgin.

SEXUAL SELF-CONTROL The ability to refrain from sexual activity.

SEXUALLY TRANSMITTED DISEASE (STD) A sexually transmitted disease (STD) is an infectious condition that is passed from one person to another during sexual activity. During sexual activity, bodily fluids and secretions are exchanged between partners. This occurs not only during vaginal intercourse, but during other sexual activity, ranging from seemingly innocuous "deep" kissing to oral and anal sex, both homosexual or heterosexual.

STANDARDS Guidelines that help a person decide what is right or wrong.

STERILITY The incapability of fertilization or reproduction.

SYPHILIS A chronic infectious disease usually venereal in origin, and can be transmitted to an unborn child. Syphilis spreads easily through the body and can affect any tissue or organ, especially the genitals, skin, mucous membranes, aorta, brain, liver, bones and nerves.

TRICHOMONIASIS An STD that affects primarily women, but men can also become infected. In women, it is considered a form of vaginitis, characterized by a persistent discharge and itching. Most men will have no symptoms, though the disease has invaded their urethra and bladder.

TUBERCULOSIS A bacterial infection which usually begins in the lungs, but may spread throughout the body. People with AIDS may be particularly susceptible to tuberculosis, often requiring complex combinations of antibiotics for treatment.

UNCONDITIONAL LOVE The unselfish respect and care for another, without sexual implications. Giving for the total good of another person.

URETHRA The thin tube which carries urine from the bladder outside the body. In men, the urethra passes through the length of the penis.

UTERUS The pear-shaped, muscular organ in the female pelvis which carries a growing baby throughout development prior to birth.

VIRGINITY Having never had sexual intercourse: a special gift one gives to their spouse in marriage.

ENDNOTES

LESSONS 1-4

1. Howard, Marion, and Judith B. McCabe, "Helping Teenagers Postpone Sexual Involvement," *Family Planning Perspective,* January/February 1990, p. 22.

2. O'Reilly, Kevin R., and Sevgi O. Aral, "Adolescence and Sexual Behavior, Trends and Implications for STD," *Journal of Adolescent Health Care,* July 1985, p. 267-268.

3. Cates, Willard, Jr., M.D., M.P.H., "Teenagers and Sexual Risk Taking: The Best of Times and the Worst of Times," *Journal of Adolescent Health,* March 1991, p. 84.

4. Anderson, John E.; Kann, Laura; Holtzman, Deborah; Arday, Susan; Truman, Ben; and Kolbe, Lloyd, "HIV/AIDS Knowledge and Sexual Behavior Among High School Students," *Family Planning Perpectives*, November/December 1990, p. 254

5. Bennett, William J., "Sex and the Education of our Children" Remarks at the National School Board Association, Washington, D.C., January 1987, p. 10.

6. Stiffman, Arlene R., Felton Earls, Lee N. Robins, Kenneth G. Jung, and Pamela Kulbok, "Adolescent Sexual Activity and Pregnancy: Socioenvironmental Problems, Physical Health, and Mental Health," *Journal of Youth and Adolescence,* October 1987.

7. Irwin, Charles E., Jr., M.D. "The Theoretical Concept of At-Risk Adolescents," *Adolescent Medicine: State of the Art Reviews,* February 1990, p. 10-11.

8. Short, Dr. Ray E. , "Sex, Love or Infatuation: How Can I Really Know?" 1980.

9. This activity was modified from an activity found in the Teen Choice's curriculum, *Reasonable Reasons To Wait.*

10. This activity was modified from an activity found in the Teen Choice's curriculum, *Reasonable Reasons To Wait.*

HIV/AIDS IN TODAY'S SOCIETY LESSON

1. "Sexual Behavior Among High School Students—United States, 1990" *MMWR (Morbidity and Mortality Weekly Report),* January 2, 1992, Vol. 40, Nos. 51 and 52. Atlanta, GA: U.S. Department of Health and Human Services, Centers for Disease Control, pp. 885-888.

2. "Rapid Progression of HIV-1 Infection to AIDS," M.B. Walsh & L.H. Calabrese, *The Cleveland Clinic Journal of Medicine,* November/December 1992, Vol. 59, No. 6, pp. 637-639.

3. "HIV Infection Is Active and Progressive in Lymphoid Tissue During the Clinically Latent Stage of Disease," Giuseppe Pantaleo, *Nature,* March 25, 1993, Vol. 362, pp. 355-358.

4. "Pre-Ejaculatory Fluid as Potential Vector for Sexual Transmission of HIV-1," J. Pudney, M. Oneta, K. Mayer, et al, *The Lancet,* December 12, 1992, Vol. 340, p. 1470.

5. "World Health Organization Says Three-Quarters of HIV Infections Transmitted Heterosexually," *WHO Press,* November 11, 1991, Geneva, Switzerland.

6. "Blood Supply Getting Safer all the Time," *AIDS Alert/Common Sense About AIDS*, 1992, 7, (5). American Health Consultants, 72B.

7. *HIV/AIDS Surveillance,* February 1993, Atlanta, GA: U.S. Department of Health and Human Services, Public Health Service, Centers for Disease Control.

8. "Pediatric AIDS in Developing Countries," *MAP International AIDS Brief,* 1993.

9. "Rate of Transmission of Human Immunodeficiency Virus Type 1 Infection from Mother to Child and Short-Term Outcome of Neonatal Infection: Results of a Prospective Cohort Study," Warren A. Andiman, et al. *American Journal of Diseases of Children,* July 1990, Vol. 144, pp. 758-766.

10. "Transmission of HIV-1 Infections from Mothers to Infants in Haiti: Impact on Childhood Mortality and Malnutrition," Neal A. Halsey, MD, et al. *Journal of the American Medical Association,* October 24/31, 1990, Vol. 264, pp. 2088-2092.

11. "The Risk of Transmission of HIV-1 Through Non-Percutaneous, Non-Sexual Modes—A Review," Robyn R.M. Gershon, et al. *AIDS,* July 1990, Vol. 4, No. 7, pp. 645-650.

12. "Risk of Human Immunodeficiency Virus Type 1 Infection Among Sexual and Nonsexual Household Contacts of Persons with Congenital Clotting Disorders," Jeanne M. Lusher, MD, et al, *Pediatrics,* August 2, 1991, Vol. 88, No. 2, pp. 242-249.

13. "HIV Cells Found in Saliva," Susan Johnson & Pat Sheridan, *Journal of the American Dental Association,* September 1991, Vol. 122, p. 69.

14. "Comparison of Female to Male and Male to Female Transmission of HIV in 563 Stable Couples: European Study Group on Heterosexual Transmission of HIV," *British Medical Journal,* March 28, 1992, Vol. 304, p. 809-813.

15. "AIDS Growing Fastest Among Women," *Chicago Tribune Company,* July 21, 1992.

16. "AIDS Warning: Peril Looms for Women," *Newsday,* July 21, 1992.

17. "Human Immunodeficiency Virus Type 1-Infected Blood Donors: Behavioral Characteristics and Reasons for Donation," L.S. Doll, L.R. Petersen, et al. *Transfusion,* 1991, Vol. 31, No. 8, pp. 704-709.

18. "Self-Disclosure of HIV Infection to Sexual Partners," Gary Marks, Ph.D., et al. *American Journal of Public Health,* October 1991, Vol. 81, No. 10, pp. 1321-1323.

19. "HIV-1 Seroprevalence and Risk Behaviors Among Young Men Who Have Sex with Other Men." Unpublished study; principle investigator, Dr. George Lemp; San Francisco/Berkeley, CA 1992-1993. Distributed by the Centers for Disease Control, Atlanta, GA.

20. "Efficacy of Nonoxynol 9 Contraceptive Sponge Use in Preventing Heterosexual Acquisition of HIV in Nairobi Prostitutes," Joan Kreiss, MD, et al. *Journal of the American Medical Association,* July 22-29, 1992, Vol. 268, No. 4, pp. 477-482.

21. "Contraceptive Failure Rates Based on the 1988 NSFG," E.F. Jones and J.D. Forrest, *Family Planning Perspectives,* January/February 1992, p. 12.

22. "A Meta-Analysis of Condom Effectiveness in Reducing Sexually Transmitted HIV," Susan C. Weller, *Social Science Medicine,* 1993, Vol. 36, No. 12, pp. 1635-1644.

23. Ibid, AIDS Alert.

24. "Simplified Enrollment for Autologous Transfusion: Automatic Referral of Presurgical Patients for Assessment for Autologous Blood Collection," S. Breanndan Moore, et al. *Mayo Clinic Proceedings,* April 1992, Vol. 67, pp. 323-327.

25. "HIV-Related Sexual Behaviors of College Students," Ann H. Butcher, et al. *Journal of American College Health,* November 1991, Vol. 40, pp. 115-118.

26. Ibid, *MAP International AIDS Brief.*

27. Ibid, *American Journal of Diseases of Children.*

28. Ibid, (See Endnote #10) *Journal of the American Medical Association,* "Transmission of Human Immunodeficiency Virus Type 1 Infection From Mother to Child and Short-Term Outcome of Neonatal Infection: Results of a Prospective Cohort Study."

29. "Helping Teenagers Postpone Sexual Involvement," Marion Howard & Judith Blamey McCabe, *Family Planning Perspectives,* January/February 1990, Vol. 22, pp. 21-26.

30. "Sex: 50 Things You Should Know Now," Kathy McCoy, *Teen Magazine,* December 1992, pp. 30-34.

31. "Impact of Perceived Social Norms on Adolescents' AIDS-Risk Behavior and Prevention," J.D. Fisher, S.J. Misovich & W.A. Fisher. In R.J. DiClemente (Ed.), *Adolescents and AIDS: A Generation in Jeopardy,* Newbury Park, CA: SAGE Publications, pp. 117-136.

Dr. Wayne Agnew
Arlington, TX
OB/Gyn

Dr. Arnold Ahnfeldt
Colorado Springs, CO
Orthopedic Surgery

Dr. Robert Albee
Dunwoody, GA
OB/Gyn

Dr. Carl E. Albertson
Plains, MT
Orthopedics

Dr. James Anderson
Midlothian, VA
Emergency Medicine

Dr. James Annest
Twin Falls, ID
Anesthesiology

Dr. Lon S. Annest
Tacoma, WA
Cardiothoracic Surgery

Dr. Stephen J. Annest
Vestal, NY
General Surgery

Dr. Douglas Appleby Jr.
Greenville, SC
Cardiovascular Surgery

Dr. Gayle W. Appleby
Greenville, SC
Pathologist

Deborah P. Armstong
Tampa, FL
Registered Nurse

Dr. Peter Armstrong
Salt Lake City, UT
Pediatric Orthopedic Surgery

Dr. Randy Armstrong
Odessa, FL
OB/Gyn

Dr. Douglas J. Arnold
Timmins, Ont
Family Practice

Dr. Edward Aston IV
San Juan Capistrano, CA
Dermatology

Dr. Clegg Austin
Murray, KY Pediatrics

Dr. James Banks
Lexington, KY
Family Practice

Dr. Evelyn R. Banks
Lexington, KY
Pathology

Dr. Jean B. Abbas
Greenville, MS
Family Practice

Dr. Howard R. Barnett
North Tonawanda, NY
Family Practice

Mrs. Jean N. Barnett
North Tonawanda, NY
Registered Nurse

Dr. Eugene J. Barth
Saint Charles, MO
Pediatrics/Internal Medicine

Dr. James Baumgartner
Dickinson, ND
Internal Medicine

Dr. Stanley C. Beachy
Carlisle, PA
OB/Gyn

Dr. Reed Bell
Gulf Breeze, FL
Pediatrics

Dr. Paul Belton Jr.
Rogers, AR
OB/Gyn

Dr. Stephen R. Belton
Sunnyvale, CA
OB/Gyn

Dr. Jonathon H. Berg
Northwood, ND
Family Practice

Dr. Mitch Bernstrom
Cedar Falls, IA
Family Practice

Dr. Currell V. Berry
Atlanta, GA
Family Practice

Dr. Marilyn M. Billingsly
St. Louis, MO
Pediatrics/Internal Medicine

Dr. M. James Black
Brownsburg, IN
Family Practice

Dr. Robert C. Blackwood
Montague, PEI
Family Practice

Dr. Ann Blemker
Vincennes, IN
Dermatology

Dr. David Blemker
Vincennes, IN
Cardiology

Dr. Peter Boelens
Vicksburg, MS
Pediatrics

Dr. Vincent E. Bolton
Kennebunkport, ME
Anesthesiology

Dr. Roger Earl Bowie
Pensacola, FL
Otolaryngology/
Head Neck Surgery

Dr. John Paul Broderson
Frankfort, KY
Ophthalmology

Dr. Tim A. Broeseker
Tallahassee, FL
Hematology/Oncology

Dr. Douglas Brooks
Olathe, KS
Family Practice

Dr. S. Dean Brown
Yukon, OK
Internal Medicine

Dr. William B. Bryan
Charlotte, NC
Pediatrics

Dr. Johnny W. Bryant
Springfield, OH
OB/Gyn

Dr. Vincent Buchinsky
Manassas, VA
Family Practice

Dr. Robert Bunge
Lexington, KY
Psychiatry

Dr. Paul Buxton
Fife, Scotland
Dermatology

Dr. David J. Cahill
Beaver, PA
Pediatrics

Dr. Lisa J. Cahill
Beaver, PA
EmergencyMedicine/
Pediatrics

Dr. Martin W. Cain
Fort Smith, AR
Diagnostic Radiology

Dr. Ron Calderisi
Vancouver, BC
General Surgery

Dr. James Cardle
Edina, MN
Pediatrics

Dr. Calvin Cargill
Lufkin, TX
Family Practice

Dr. Byron H. Carlson
Forest City, IA
Family Practice

Dr. Gregory Carter
Gadsden, AL
Urology

Dr. James S. Ceton
Grand Haven, MI
General Surgery

Dr. G. Summers Chaffin
Hendersonville, TN
Family Practice

Dr. Albert T. H. Chan
Lakeland, FL
Gastroenterology

Dr. Steven T. Chen
Lancaster, PA
Gastroenterology/
Internal Medicine

Dr. Brian Clarke
Indianapolis, IN
Gastroenterology

Dr. Renita B. Clarke
Indianapolis, IN
Infectious Diseases

Dr. Christopher Claydon
Grass Valley, CA
Family Practice

Dr. Daniel Clemens
New Philadelphia, OH
Ophthalmology

Dr. James L. Clemens
Orange City, IA
Family Practice

Dr. James Clements Jr.
Pensacola, FL
Infectious Diseases

Dr. Beth A. Colonna
San Antonio, TX
Anesthesiology

Dr. Joseph R. Contarino
Ooltewah, TN
Emergency Medicine

Dr. Margaret M. Cottle
Vancouver, BC
Family Practice/
Palliative Care

Dr. Robin W. Cottle
Vancouver, BC
Ophthalmology

Dr. John Crawford
Birmingham, AL
Emergency Medicine

Dr. Burns Creighton
Tampa, FL
Ophthalmology

Dr. Anton Crepinsek Jr.
Cabot, AR
Family Practice

Dr. David L. Dalton
Tyler, TX
OB/Gyn

Dr. Thomas E. Daniel
Redding, CA
Orthopedic Surgery

Dr. Mary Davenport
Berkely, CA
Orthopedic Surgery

Dr. Arthur S. Davis
Manteca, CA
Orthopedic Surgery

Dr. Alex DeJong
Orland Park, IL
Family Practice

Dr. Joel DeKoning
Wausau, WI
OB/Gyn

Dr. Paul DePriest
Lexington, KY
Gynecologic Oncology

Dr. V.G. Dickson
Cannington, ONT
General Practice

Dr. Albert C. Diddams
Colorado Springs, CO
General Surgery

Dr. Daniel Diehl
Willow Sreet, PA
Family Practice

Dr. Kent Donovan
Deerborn, MI
Radiology

Dr. Allen R. Doran
Roseville, CA
Psychiatry

Dr. Mark Drogowski
Cheboygan, MI
Family Practice

Dr. Deborah Drovdal
Great Falls, MT
Diagnostic Radiology

Dr. Daryl Dutter
Modesto, CA
Family Practice

Dr. Joseph W. Eades
St. Louis, MO
Plastic Surgery

Dr. Arthur D. Earl
Salmon, ID
Family Practice

Dr. Marvin E. Eastlund
Fort Wayne, IN
OB/Gyn

Dr. Doug Eaton
Riverside, CA
Internal Medicine

Dr. Russ Engevik
Julian, CA
Emergency Medicine

Dr. Jack England
Sedalia, CO
Emergency Medicine
Family Practice

Dr. Kent Erb
Sheridan, IN
Family Practice

Dr. Gregory Erena
Lexington, KY
Oral/Maxillofacial Surgery

Dr. Craig R. Evans
Edmond, OK
Family Practice

Dr. William R. Faust
Tampa, FL
Family Practice

Dr. Joyce Fischer
Bluffton, IN
Pediatrics

Dr. James D. Fitz
Tacoma, WA
Internal Medicine

Dr. Ernest Fletcher
Lexington, KY
Family Practice

Dr. Dennis N. Floyd
Springdale, AR
Anesthesiology

Dr. Diane Foley
Indianapolis, IN
Pediatrics

Dr. Steve Foley
Indianapolis, IN
OB/Gyn

Dr. Carl L. Fugate
Beloit, KS
Family Practice

Dr. Ernest Fuller
Melfort, SK
General Surgery

Dr. Lori Fuller
Melfort, SK
Anesthesiology

Dr. Robert Fulmer
Austin, TX
Gynecology

Dr. Ralph Gage
Colorado Springs, CO
Family Practice

Dr. Peter J. Ganzer Jr.
Eagan, MN
Internal Medicine

Dr. Stephen Genuis
Sherwood Park, AB
OB/Gyn

Dr. Larry Gerbens
Grand Rapids, MI
Ophthalmology

Dr. Jack Geren
Lexington, KY
Emergency Medicine

Dr. James H. Getzen
Arcadia, CA
Cardiology

Dr. David Gieser
Wheaton, IL
Ophthalmology

Dr. James B. Gillick
Poulsbo, WA
Internal Medicine

Dr. Gordon Golden
Colorado Springs, CO
Internal Medicine

Dr. H. Leon Greene
Woodinville, WA
Cardiology

Dr. Chris Griffith
Olympia, WA
General Surgery

Dr. Curtis A. Groote
Rapid City, SD
Otolaryngology

Dr. Raymond S. Gruby
Bismark, ND
Orthopedic Surgery

Dr. Ed G. Guttery III
Ft. Myers, FL
Pediatrics

Dr. Gary Haakenson
Raleigh, NC
OB/Gyn

Dr. David Hager
Lexington, KY
OB/Gyn

Dr. Mitchell A. Harris
Fishers, IN
Pediatrics

Dr. Tim Harstad
Pewaukee, WI
OB/Gyn

Dr. John Hartman
Kissimmee, FL
Family Practice

Dr. Charles Hayden
Austin, TX
Psychiatry

Dr. John Heavrin
Lakewood, CO
OB/Gyn

Dr. Craig P. Hedges
Sioux Falls, SD
Otolaryngology

Dr. Lee T. Helms
Roanoke, VA
Ophthalmology

Dr. Gordon E. Henneford
Billings, MT
Otolaryngology

Dr. Linda Hernandez
San Antonio, TX
Family Practice

Dr. Jacqueline J. Herold
Bronte, TX
Emergency Medicine

Dr. James S. Hicks
Rock Hill, SC
Family Practice

Dr. Lewis Hicks
Lexington, KY
OB/Gyn

Dr. Jeffery Hillesland
La Crosse, WI
Emergency Medicine

Dr. John Hilsenbeck Jr.
Memphis, TN
Pathology

Dr. Earl C. Hoffer
Pampa, TX
Family Practice

Dr. Jeff Hoffsommer
Okeene, OK
Family Practice

Dr. James W. Hogin
Oklahoma City, OK
Internal Medicine

Dr. M. Lance Holemon
Scottsdale, AZ
OB/Gyn

Dr. Charles Holland Jr.
Bartlesville, OK
Otolaryngology

Dr. Kathleen Holland
Kerrville, TX
Pediatrics

Dr. Ripley Hollister
Colorado Springs, CO
Family Practice

Dr. Scott Horn
San Antonio, TX
Family Practice

Dr. Mark S. Hoppe
Plains, MT
Family Practice

Dr. Roy S. Horras
Oak Park, IL
Emergency Medicine

Dr. Barry L. Huey
Spartanburg, SC
Cardiology

Dr. David L. Hunter
Peoria, IL
Diagnostic Neuroradiology

Dr. C. Max Hutchinson
Tupelo, MS
Cardiothoracic Surgery

Dr. Wilmer Iler
Van Wert, OH
Family Practice

Dr. Richard Ingle
Winnemucca, NV
Family Practice

Dr. Donald Jasper
Sacramento, CA
Family Practice

Dr. William J. John
Lexington, KY
Internal Medicine

Dr. Ben Johnson
Colorado Springs, CO
Family Practice

Dr. Scott W. Johnson
Duluth, MN
OB/Gyn

Dr. Theodore Johnstone
Fresno, CA
Family Practice

Dr. D. Brynley Jones
Platte, SD
Family Practice

Dr. Calvin Jones
Baltimore, MD
Vascular Surgery

Dr. Gary R. Jones
Austin, TX
OB/Gyn

Dr. Lyle Joyce
Plymouth, MN
Cardiac Surgery

Dr. W. R. Julien
Summerland, BC
Family Practice/Anesthesia

Dr. Stephen Jurco III
Austin, TX
Pathology

Dr. Dick L. Kamps
Muskegon, MI
General Surgery

Dr. Allan G. Kavalich
Redlands, CA
Nephrology/Internal
Medicine

Dr. Lawrence Kelley
Maitland, FL
Family Practice

Dr. Richard A. Kempf
Holland, MI
Family Practice

Dr. G.M. Kelton
Timmins, ONT
Family Practice

Dr. Robert Kinney
Concord, NC
Pathology

Dr. Lee E. Krauth
Evergreen, CO
Neurosurgery

Dr. Robert A. LaFleur
Grand Rapids, MI
Emergency Medicine

Dr. Charles D. Langford
Lafayette, LA
Surgery/Oncology

Dr. David L. Larson
Elm Grove, WI
Plastic Surgery

Dr. George V. Lawry II
Iowa City, IA
Internal Medicine

Dr. Bill R. Lee
Ennis, TX
Family Practice

Dr. Jan Lee
Wichita Falls, TX
Family Practice

Dr. Paul W. Leithart
Columbus, OH
Family Practice

Dr. Richard Liliedahl
Temecula, CA
Family Practice

Dr. John P. Livoni
Sacramento, CA
Radiology

Dr. Susan C. Loeffel
Hasting, NE
Pathologist

Dr. Robert B. Love
Madison, WI
Thoracic Surgery

Dr. James Lovell
San Antonio, TX
OB/Gyn

Dr. Roger Loven
Bismarck, ND
Anesthesiology

Dr. D. Andrew MacFarlan
Earlysville, VA
Family Practice

Dr. Robert W. Mann
Arlington, TX
Pediatrics

Dr. Wayne A. Marlowe
Nicholasville, KY
Family Practice

Mrs. Cynthia Martin
West Linn, OR
Registered Nurse

Dr. Daniel Martin
Erin, TN
Family Practice

Dr. Randall L. Martin
West Linn, OR
Anesthesiology

Dr. Michael W. Mathews
Olathe, KS
Family Practice

Dr. Kevin S. Maxwell
Grass Valley, CA
Family Practice

Dr. Louis McBurney
Marble, CO
Psychiatry

Dr. Deborah McClain
Tucker, GA
Anesthesiology

Dr. Rebecca L. McClarren
Wauseon, OH
Family Practice

Dr. Chris McCoy
Owensboro, KY
Vascular Surgery

Dr. Leroy McCune
Orchard Park, NY
Family Practice

Dr. George McIlhaney
College Station, TX
Family Practice

Dr. William P. McKay
Dalton, GA
Radiation Oncology

Dr. Warren McKelvy
Roswell, NM
Pediatrics

Dr. Timothy McKone
Salt Lake City, UT
General Surgery

Dr. John McMurray
Kingsport, TN
Diagnostic Radiology

Dr. Benjamin McWilliams
Ft. Worth, TX
OB/Gyn

Dr. Paul Meier
Dallas, TX
Psychiatry

Dr. Carl Meyer
Greenville, PA
Pediatrics

Dr. Kathryn R. Meyer
Greenville, PA
Emergency Medicine

Dr. Joe Milan
Bloomington, IN
General Surgery

Dr. D. Brett Mitchell
Benbrook, TX
Family Practice

Dr. Sharon L. Moellenhoff
Los Angeles, CA
Pediatrics/Anesthiologêy

Dr. Robert Moore
Pineville, LA
Family Practice

Dr. Rebecca Moorhead
Jacksonville, FL
OB/Gyn

Dr. M. Montgomery
Emporia, KS
Orthopedic Surgery

Dr. Mark W. Muilenburg
Orange City, IA
Family Practice

Dr. Kent R. Murphy
Monument, CO
Head/Neck Surgery

Dr. Richard Myers
Jacksonville, FL
OB/Gyn

Dr. Nadine Nakazono
Castle Rock, CO
Family Practice

Dr. Britt Nelson
Fort Worth, TX
Pediatric Critical Care

118

Dr. Donald Nelson
Cedar Rapids, IA
Family Practice

Dr. Mary Nelson
Cedar Rapids, IA
Family Practice

Dr. John A. Newcomer
Colorado Springs, CO
Pulmonary/Critical Care
Medicine

Dr. Matthew Newman
Tacoma, WA
Emergency Medicine

Dr. Leslie Newton
Seattle, WA
Family Practice

Phyllis J. Newton
Seattle, WA
Registered Nurse

Dr. Michael Noel
Houston, TX
Family Practice

Dr. Ross Olson
Minneapolis, MN
Pediatrics

Dr. Kirk D. Pagel
Moreno Valley, CA
Family Practice

Dr. Steven E. Parnell
Fairmont, MN
Family Practice

Dr. David Pate
Mobile, AL
Internal Medicine

Dr. William Peinhardt
Cullman, AL
Internist

Dr. M. Dale Perrigan
Crossville, TN
OB/Gyn

Dr. R.M. Peterson
Great Falls, MT
Emergency Medicine

Dr. D.W. Pettigrew III
Watkinsville, GA
Emergency Medicine

Dr. Terrence A. Pheifer
Kirkland, WA
OB/Gyn

Dr. Westell Phelan
Steamboat Springs, CO
Diagnostic Radiology

Dr. Steve E. Phurrough
Colorado Springs, CO
Family Practice

Dr. Robert Pinkston
Amarillo, TX
Radiology

Dr. Gregory A. Poland
Rochester, MN
Internal Medicine

Dr. Jerry Popham
Lakewood, CO
Ophthalmic Plastic Surgery

Dr. Mark A. Povich
Minot, ND
Family Practice

Dr. Scott M. Pratho
Aledo, TX
Emergency Medicine

Dr. Larry Puls
Amarillo, TX
OB/Gyn

Dr. Jerry S. Putman
Tyler, TX
OB/Gyn

Dr. Richard L. Putnam
Escondido, CA
Family Practice

Dr. Frank R. Raymond
Dublin, OH
OB/Gyn

Dr. George Rapp
Indianapolis, IN
Orthopedic Surgery

Dr. Samuel Ravenel
High Point, NC
Pediatrics

Dr. Sheri Reinhard-Doe
Bartlesville, OK
Family Practice

Dr. William D. Reynolds
Tampa, FL
Ophthalmology

Dr. Drew D. Ritter
Austin, CO
Orthopedic Surgery

Dr. David Roberts
Columbus, GA
OB/Gyn

Dr. Douglas Robinson
San Antonio, TX
General Surgery

Dr. David Rollins
Turlock, CA
Family Practice

Dr. Michael Rothman
Santa Fe, NM
Orthopedic Surgery

Dr. Paul D. Rothwell
Bethany, OK
Family Practice

Dr. Jeffery Sabine
Oklahoma City, OK
Family Practice

Dr. James K. Saiki
Bakersfield, CA
Internal Medicine

Dr. Richard Samuel
Ellensburg, WA
Family Practice

Dr. & Mrs. Web Sandbulte
Issaquah, WA
Orthopedic Surgeon

Dr. Elizabeth Sanford
Tacoma, WA
OB/Gyn

Dr. Perry M. Santos
Springfield, IL
Otolaryngology/
Head Neck Surgery

Dr. Stephen Sawada
Indianapolis, IN
Cardiology

Dr. Arthur E. Schmidt
Cedar Falls, IA
Internal Medicine

Dr. Charles Setterstrom
Grand Rapids, MI
Pediatrics

D. Jeffrey P. Shafer
Geneva, IL
Radiation Oncology

Dr. David Shahian
Sudbury, MA
Cardiothoracic Surgery

Dr. James H. Sheerin
Pensacola, FL
Cardiology

Dr. David D. Shilling
Mount Vernon, WA
Family Practice

Dr. Michael Shipley
Durham, NC
Internal Medicine

Dr. Orman W. Simmons
Little Rock, AR
OB/Gyn

Dr. Dorsett Smith
Everett, WA
Pulmonary Disease

Dr. Steven Smith
Carmel, IN
Occupational/Environmental
Medicine

Dr. Marshall Sorensen
Selma, CA
Family Practice

Dr. John Spore
Mountain Home, AR
General Surgery

Dr. Curtis C. Stine
Denver, CO
Family Practice

Dr. Roy Stringfellow
Colorado Springs, CO
OB/Gyn

Dr. David Subich
Mansfield, OH
Internal Medicine

Dr. Steven Suits
Spartanburg, SC
Pediatric Surgery

Dr. Patrick D. Sura
Superior, WI
Family Practice

Dr. Howard Swanson
Marshfield, WI
Rheumatology

Dr. Scott C. Swim
Indianapolis, IN
Otolaryagology/
Head Neck Surgery

Dr. Byron Tabbut
Warrenville, IL
Ophthalmology

Dr. James M. Taylor
Beavercreek, OH
Family Practice

Dr. Mark Taylor
Colleyville, TX
Family Practice

Dr. Zack Taylor
Germantown, TN
Gastoenterology

Dr. William Terpstra
Carmel, IN
Family Practice

Dr. Michael H. Terry
Great Falls, MT
Family Practice

Dr. John Thesing
Leawood, KS
Gastoenterology

Dr. Bodo Treu
Storm Lake, IA
Family Practice

Dr. Christopher M. Tsoi
Fort Collins, CO
Plastic/Reconstructive
Surgery

Dr. A. Gregory Tuegel
Abilene, TX
Pediatrics

Health Professional Endorsements

Dr. Fred T. Tuttle
Georgetown, KY
Family Practice

Dr. Carl VanderKooi
Cedar Falls, IA
Internal Medicine

Dr. David VanGorp
Orange City, IA
Family Practice

Dr. John Vasko
Seattle, WA
Radiology

Dr. Marvin Vaughan
Rochester, MN
Internal Medicine

Gay Vela, Ph.D.
Lincoln, NE PhD
Univ. of Nebraska

Dr. Frank G. Veres
Warren, OH
Family Practice

Dr. Hendrik Visser
Crapaud, PEI
Family Practice

Dr. Scott Voorman
Thousand Oaks, CA
Otolaryngology

Dr. F. Dennis Waldron
Gig Harbor, WA
Internal Medicine/
Gastroenterology

Dr. Hal Wallis
Waxahachie, TX
OB/Gyn

Dr. Ben Warf
Lexington, KY
Pediatric Neurosurgery

Dr. Gary L. Weber
Linden, WI
Cardiology

Dr. Peter M. Webster
Toronto, ONT
Internal Medicine

Dr. Chris Wells
Roanoke, VA
Cardiovascular/Thoracic
Surgery

Mrs. Eleanor Wells
Roanoke, VA
Registered Nurse

Dr. E. Wenthe Jr.
Springfield, IL
Family Practice

Dr. Thomas E. Wex
Madison, WI
Family Practice

Dr. Robin White
Reno, NV
Pediatrics

Dr. James C. Wilkes
Lexington, KY
Pediatrics

Dr. Kenneth Williams Jr.
Santa Ana, CA
Family Practice

Dr. Nancy J. Williams
Saint Louis, MO
Internal Medicine

Dr. Peter J. Williams
Boerne, TX
Podiatry

Dr. Robert Williams
Selah, WA
Gastroentecology/Internal
Medicine

Dr. Malcolm E. Williamson
Grosse Ile, MI
Endocrinology/Nuclear
Medicine

Dr. Bob Willis
Hendersonville, TN
Otoloryngology

Mrs. Susan L. Willis
Hendersonville, TN
Pharmacist

Dr. Franklin D. Wilson
Indianapolis, IN
Orthopedic Surgeon

Dr. John Witherington
Memphis, TN
Internal Medicine/
Emergency Medicine

Dr. Thomas E. Witzig
Rochester, MN
Hematology/Uncology

Mrs. Diane Witzig
Rochester, MN
Registered Nurse

Dr. David Wolf
Trenton, MI
OB/Gyn

Dr. Brian D. Wolfe
Iola, KS
Family Practice

Dr. E. Jane Woolley
Glendale, CA
Anethesiology

Dr. Morton M. Woolley
Los Angeles, CA
Pediatric Surgery

Dr. Dennis Worthington
Paradise, CA
Family Practice

Dr. Thomas J. Yetman
Muskegon, MI
OB/Gyn

Dr. John Yezerski
Murray, KY
Orthopedic Surgery

Dr. Richard H. Yook
Woodland Hills, CA
Ophthalmology

Dr. Corinne Zamonsky
Calgary, ALTA
Family Practice

Dr. Anne Zimmerman
Casper, WY
General Surgery

Notes

Notes

Notes